T0087196

Write No Matter What

....

Chicago Guides
to *Writing*, Editing,
and Publishing

Write
No Matter What

ADVICE FOR ACADEMICS

Joli Jensen

THE UNIVERSITY OF CHICAGO PRESS

Chicago and London

The University of Chicago Press, Chicago 60637
The University of Chicago Press, Ltd., London

For more information, contact the University of Chicago Press,
1427 E. 60th St., Chicago, IL 60637.
Published 2017

Printed in the United States of America

26 25 24 23 22 21   6

ISBN-13: 978-0-226-46167-0 (cloth)
ISBN-13: 978-0-226-46170-0 (paper)
ISBN-13: 978-0-226-46184-7 (e-book)
DOI: 10.7208/chicago/9780226461847.001.0001

Library of Congress Cataloging-in-Publication Data

Names: Jensen, Joli, author.
Title: Write no matter what : advice for academics / Joli Jensen.
Other titles: Chicago guides to writing, editing, and publishing.
Description: Chicago : The University of Chicago Press, 2017. | Series: Chicago
    guides to writing, editing, and publishing | Includes bibliographical references
    and index.
Identifiers: LCCN 2016048009 | ISBN 9780226461670 (cloth : alk. paper) |
    ISBN 9780226461700 (pbk. : alk. paper) | ISBN 9780226461847 (e-book)
Subjects: LCSH: Academic writing.
Classification: LCC LB2369 .J46 2017 | DDC 808.02—dc23 LC record available at
    https://lccn.loc.gov/2016048009

♾ This paper meets the requirements of ANSI/NISO Z39.48-1992
(Permanence of Paper).

In memory of my father,

DONALD D. JENSEN

(1930–2003)

CONTENTS

. . . .

ACKNOWLEDGMENTS

· ·

The University of Tulsa has given me the institutional support I needed to create and direct the TU Faculty Writing Program. In particular, I want to thank Denise Dutton, director of the Henneke Center for Academic Fulfillment, for her encouragement, advice, and administrative skills, as well as Provost Roger Blais, Dean Kalpana Misra, Lauren Wagner, and Janet Cairns.

My departmental colleagues Mark Brewin, John Coward, and Ben Peters have graciously accepted my increasing commitment to faculty writing, and Ben's enthusiasm for this project has been particularly encouraging.

The seeds of this book go way back. I thank the graduate students I worked with in the Radio-TV-Film Department at the University of Texas, as well as undergraduate students in the TU Honors Program, for sharing their writing struggles with me. This book began thanks to a passing remark from historian Ed Linenthal, visiting from Indiana University. He told me I should turn a class handout called "Myths We Stall By" into a book. Never underestimate the power of an encouraging word.

I have received many encouraging words during the writing of this book. In particular I want to thank my TU colleagues Jennifer Airey, Susan Chase, Lynn Clutter, Lars Engle, Eduardo Faingold, Randy Fuller, Al Harkness, Brian Hosmer, Jennie Ikuta, Holly Laird, Peggy Lisenbee, Lee Anne Nichols, Kristen Oertel, Kirsten Olds, Teresa Valero, Kate Waits, and Helen Zhang for their support, along with the TU colleagues I consulted with in confidence. Outside of TU, Rabbi Marc Boone Fitzerman, CSU Writes! founder Kristina Quynn, Ray Blanton, Karen Christensen, David D. Perlmutter, and Sue Redwood have offered valued encouragement.

Thanks also go to Vitae, the *Chronicle of Higher Education*'s online career hub, especially to editor Gabriela Montell, for the chance to circulate some of these ideas in essay form.

The University of Chicago Press has been an ideal home for this project. It has been gratifying to work with editors David Morrow and Mary Laur, along with editorial associate Susan Zakin, manuscript editor Ruth Goring, production controller Skye Agnew, designer Kevin Quach, and promotions manager Lauren Salas.

I am grateful to have grown up in a family that values scholarly writing. I thank my mother, Janet Kepner Jensen, for her lifetime of support. As this book took shape, I was especially buoyed by my brother Michael Jensen's insights on academic publishing and my brother David Jensen's insights on writing in the sciences. This book is dedicated to the memory of our father, Donald D. Jensen, who inspired all of us and encouraged me to find ways around writing obstacles.

Finally, I am deeply grateful for the love (and copyediting) of my husband, Craig Walter, and our sons Charlie Walter and Tom Walter. They continue to encourage me, even though I sometimes shut the door on them (at least for a few hours a day) in order to write.

Readers are invited to visit my webpage: jolijensen.com.

PREFACE

· ·

Writing productivity research and advice can be summarized in a single sentence: In order to be productive we need frequent, low-stress contact with a writing project we enjoy. Our problem is that academic life offers us the exact opposite: infrequent, high-stress contact with projects that come to feel like albatrosses.

Outsiders think academe is a supportive writing environment. We know it is not. Yes, we have semester breaks and time off in the summer, and we meet with only a few classes each day, but we are in a hectic, demanding, distracting work environment that is definitely not writing-friendly. Academe sets the stakes very high (publish or perish) while mystifying the writing process. We are expected to figure out—all on our own—how to publish prolifically, teach well, and be of service to students and colleagues.

It is up to us to create better conditions to support our writing—to find ways to have frequent, rewarding contact with enjoyable projects. But first we need to stop blaming our situation or ourselves. Academic life is unsupportive to writing for reasons beyond our legitimate complaints about having too much to do or our secret fears about being lazy and undisciplined. There are insights we can have, and skills we can develop, that will help us do our academic writing no matter what.

In this book I focus on the process of academic writing rather than on the content. There are already many useful books on writing style and on the publication process for academic articles or books. This book is about dealing with whatever is keeping you from getting your academic writing done. It shows you how to create and sustain frequent, low-stress writing contact with a project you care about, no matter how stuck you are, frustrated you feel, or uncongenial your writing environment seems.

In the following pages, I ask you to let go of the fantasy that you need to be somewhere else, or become someone else, in order to write productively. I ask you to stop beating yourself up for not already knowing how to write happily and often. I ask you to stop blaming teaching and service (as well as students and colleagues) for filling your time and draining your energy. When we let go of our rationalizations, we free ourselves to address the obstacles that really stand in our way.

In the sections that follow I draw on popular and scholarly insights on what hinders, as well as supports, the writing process. I combine these with my own writing struggles and insights from thirty-plus years as a professor, along with what I've learned from developing and directing a writing program for faculty at the University of Tulsa. The techniques and suggestions I offer here are helping colleagues in a variety of humanities, social and behavioral sciences, and scientific disciplines at my university and elsewhere. Yes, we academics work in a particularly challenging writing environment, but it really is possible to write happily and productively in academe. In the following pages I tell you how.

Part One

WRITING IN ACADEME

1} LETTING GO OF THE DREAM

. . . .

Many of us were drawn to academic life because we yearned to live "the life of the mind." We hoped to spend quiet hours thinking great thoughts while discovering important things. We imagined having creative and supportive colleagues and plenty of time to talk with them about our ideas. The movies show professors having deep conversations in wood-paneled offices or taking contemplative walks between classes down ivy-covered lanes. No wonder outsiders assume that we have plenty of time to write! If only.

Even though we realize that this image is a fantasy, we may still cling to some version of it. We know that our current situation feels writing-deflective, even perhaps writing-hostile. We hope that once we land a tenure-track job, or get tenure, or become a full professor, it will be easier to find ways to write. Or maybe if we get to a "better" university we will find more support for our scholarship. It is easy to keep yearning for an academic utopia, somewhere we can be productive, valued, and supported.

That's certainly what I yearned for. Even though I was surrounded by evidence that universities weren't at all like the dreams in my head or the images in the movies (and I was a media studies scholar, and my father was a professor!), I kept seeking that book-lined study in the company of supportive colleagues, with ample time to read, write and think. Someday I would have just what I needed to write lots, easily and well. The struggle would finally be over, and I would live in an academic arcadia.

Eventually I realized that my actual situation was never going to match my dreams. This allowed me to face reality—if I wanted to write, then I needed to find ways to write productively in the real academic world. Once I stopped blaming my circumstances, I was able to find ways to secure reliable writing time, space, and energy. I learned how to recognize and find ways around the writing myths that kept me anxious and miserable.

For far too many of us, academic writing is a perplexing burden, a source of constant anxiety, self-doubt, and confusion. The entry stakes are very high—publish or perish. But even after tenure the writing stakes continue to be daunting. Our self-respect, as well as the respect of our peers, depends on our ability to keep writing. We know that scholarly productivity is the constant coin of our realm, yet most of us struggle mightily in our efforts to accrue enough of it.

We may have spurts of productivity alternating with excruciating droughts. Or we may dutifully (but resentfully) concoct yet another essay or article in a corner of the field that feels less and less interesting to us. We may apply for grants knowing we have to get them to keep our funding, while half-hoping we won't get them so we don't have to deal with too many projects at once and more rounds of deadlines and revisions.

We come up with avoidance strategies that work all too well until we are faced with professional reviews, and then we crank out what we can, quickly and sullenly. No matter how many lines we add to our CV, we can still feel like we are missing the mark. The tragic truth of academic life is that everyone I know is constantly trying to be more productive while feeling anxiety and shame about not writing "enough."

I spent years wondering what I was doing wrong—why wasn't I writing more, and more happily, while still having time and energy for teaching, service, family, and friends? Why wasn't this working out like it was "supposed" to? I recognized, dimly, that I was in the grip of a fantasy about what academic life can be and that I didn't know how to write effectively in academic reality.

I didn't want to become bitter, and I didn't want to become "deadwood"—a professor who doesn't publish and therefore should be pruned from the departmental tree. This is a cruel but common way to describe tenured colleagues who may still have much to offer but, because they are not actively writing, are treated with disdain.

We are surrounded by cautionary examples of what happens when writing doesn't go well. There are the colleagues who are not publishing anything but refuse to do service because they claim that they still "need time to write." There are the colleagues who do their writing and publishing with grim determination, joylessly. And there are the colleagues who talk confidently about their project's progress even after it has become painfully clear to everyone else that little or no writing is actually being done. In this brackish and judgmental climate, few of us deal realistically with our writing; few of us are able to acknowledge how it is actually going or how we really feel about it.

The less I was able to approximate my academic fantasy, the more betrayed I felt. I was stuck in the gap between what I yearned for and what I was actually experiencing. And that was with a fortunate academic career, begun in a field that was growing just as I received my PhD from a respected graduate program. Thanks to timing as much as ability, I have taught at three good universities and have been tenured and promoted without excessive trauma, all while writing and publishing books, chapters, and articles. From the outside, I'm sure it looked like I was living the academic dream, almost effortlessly.

But I was not. I was blocked for many months before finally finding some helpful productivity techniques that allowed me to write my dissertation. Since then I have started many writing projects that mysteriously stalled and so eventually had to be painfully abandoned. I have tried all kinds of "carrot and stick" schemes to get myself to write, but few of them worked for very long. I have been mired in collaborative writing projects that frustrated and drained me, keeping me from working on what really interested me.

Even when writing was going reasonably well, I agonized over how writing takes precious time away from family, friends, and everything else life has to offer. I felt drawn and quartered as I struggled to find that popular chimera: work-life balance. I was stressed and rushed when writing, and stressed and rushed when not writing. Where was my longed-for "life of the mind"? I questioned the point of it all—was it really worth it?

This book is the outgrowth of my own desire to find ways out of my misery, as well as my desire to be of help to valued colleagues whose careers are at risk because of their unresolved writing issues. My father's scholarly life was shadowed by a long-deflected (and ultimately abandoned) contract for a seminal introductory textbook. Several faculty members in my own small department have been denied tenure because they claimed all was going well until it was too late for them to address or overcome their writing obstacles.

One of the interesting paradoxes of academic life is that the traditional academic schedule offers us tantalizing little slices of our "life of the mind" fantasy. One reason it is hard for us to face the reality of our situation is that we actually have research days, weekends, winter breaks, summers, and sabbaticals. This makes our writing issues even more mystifying and shaming. To our dismay, we discover that even when we have these enviable bits of "time off," we still fail to get writing done.

During breaks, summers, and sabbaticals we find ourselves getting ready to write but never quite getting there; or reading but not actually writing; or writing in circles without much progress; or revising but not submitting or resubmitting. At the end of our guilt-ridden "free" time we may finally force ourselves to write in a frantic binge as deadlines loom and our classes are about to start. This means that we are (once again) doing the very opposite of what works: we are spending infrequent, high-stress, low-reward time on a project that we just want to be rid of.

No wonder it is so hard for us to write! We have learned to produce grudgingly, in fits and starts, under relentless pressure, with an academic sword of Damocles (deadlines or tenure or professional reviews) hanging over our heads. This is both tragic and unnecessary. Our scholarly writing can be done without guilt, pressure, or shame. We can deploy effective writing techniques, bust the myths that keep us from writing, find ways to keep going when our momentum flags, and create the writing support we need and deserve. That is what I cover in the chapters that follow.

2 } DEMYSTIFYING ACADEMIC WRITING

. . . .

For generations we have wrapped academic writing in mystery—keeping quiet about our own writing issues and publicly shaming those who visibly struggle with theirs. This has to change. Our trouble with writing is not evidence of our unfitness for the profession. It is not some secret sign of unworthiness or ineptitude. It is nothing to be ashamed of.

When our writing isn't happening, we need to become willing to admit this and ask for help. Writing involves a particular set of practices that can be mastered and shared. If academic writing is a craft that can be learned, then we need to be doing a much better job of helping ourselves—and each other—learn how to practice our craft. That is the only way we can break through the silence and shame that has kept so many of us from figuring out how to be productive scholars.

Every step of the way we can acknowledge that academic writing is psychologically and emotionally challenging for all of us. It is not "just you" who is having trouble, and it is not "your fault" that it is hard. Each of us can benefit from requesting and using the writing guidance and advice of our colleagues. But sadly, the academic environment rarely offers support for this central, and most challenging, element of our professional life.

Rightly or wrongly, the measure of our professional worth continues to be our ability to write and get published. Writing and publishing is how we gain status and attention as graduate students, how we win postdocs or entry-level positions, how we become eligible for tenure-track positions, and finally—if we are fortunate—how we achieve tenure. And then it remains the way we keep the respect of our colleagues, as well as how we measure our own professional standing and accomplishments.

But the challenge goes beyond this. When we run into writing trouble, we are afraid to ask for the writing guidance that might be out there. Our advisors and mentors, the people who could help us learn how to do academic writing more easily, are also people who might punish us for not knowing how to do it already. As graduate students and untenured faculty members, we can't afford to take the risk. Won't it just make things worse to ask for help?

As our careers progress and we become tenured and potential mentors ourselves, we still don't want to admit that we are often flying blind, muddling through as best we can, becoming disheartened or desperate. Sometimes we manage to find our way around self-created and system-created writing obstacles and into print, but not always, and never "enough." Even the most prolific and successful of us feel that we need to keep our writing struggles under wraps.

Writing issues don't just disappear by themselves, and surrounding them in fear and mystery only makes things worse. It is reprehensible that graduate students are supposed to figure out, apparently by osmosis, how to master the writing process, then submit and publish like a senior professor, or that a postdoc or tenure-track faculty member is expected to already know the writing/publication ropes. Asking for guidance at any juncture risks giving the impression that you don't have the right stuff—"if you need writing advice, then maybe you don't really belong here."

Given this mystification process, a tenured faculty member who runs into writing trouble will disguise it as long as possible. Making it to tenure does not mean that writing issues have been mastered; it just means that writing obstacles haven't yet become overwhelming. In fact, because of the shame we've attached to "being unproductive," few tenured faculty members will admit to experiencing writing problems of any kind. So the academic writing process stays mystified even for many senior faculty members, as well as for the students and junior colleagues they could and should be able to mentor.

Very few of us are lucky enough to have advisors who honestly share what actually goes into most writing: self-doubt, fear, frustration, avoidance, stalling, redrafting, revising, resubmitting, getting rejected, trying again. Even productive colleagues may not be able to tell you how they manage to write in spite of and through their own obstacles. They may not know what techniques are most helpful or what the research says about sustaining academic productivity. They may not have a clue about how to help you when things go awry—as things so often do.

So if you want to become a happy and productive academic writer, you will need to be willing to train yourself. You need to learn and use basic writing-support techniques, and you need to commit to getting past your own self-created obstacles. Two books that have been particularly helpful to me are Robert Boice's *Professors as Writers* (1990) and Paul J. Silvia's *How to Write a Lot* (2010); their insights are threaded through the pages that follow.

Make a commitment to taking your writing struggles seriously—take them out of the shadows and into the light. Don't fall for the myth that writing just happens for those lucky few who have the right academic stuff. Pretending that all is well just makes things worse for you and for others. We may not be able to change the extremely high stakes of academic writing, and we may not be able to reduce the nature and number of conflicting demands our jobs put on us. But we can find ways to acknowledge our writing struggles and then discover and use writing productivity techniques that really work.

3 } CRAFTSMAN ATTITUDE

....

raftsmanship is the concept that can stabilize us when we feel buffeted by academic anxieties. Treating our writing as a craft reminds us that scholarship is always, at least in part, an apprenticeship. It keeps us in touch with the fact that academic writing is something we can learn how to do. Our job (as with any craft) is to gather and deploy effective tools to help us develop from clumsy amateurs into ever-more skilled professionals.

Academics can be uncomfortable with the craftsman metaphor. Perhaps because being a successful student (and professor) requires looking and sounding smart, we learn how to offer impressive intellectual performances while hiding our clumsiness and ineptitude. This means we may see our writing as a test of our ability to impress, rather than express. It may feel humiliating to patiently work on the gradual building of productive writing skills and techniques.

In academic life we live by our wits, a colleague once told me. He meant that we rely almost solely on our mental abilities to succeed. Like con artists and performers, we become experts in appearances, acting like we always know what we are doing, pretending we are better than we are. This is the opposite of the craftsman attitude, which involves instead an honest commitment to learning how to do better and better work. The ethic of craftsmanship involves a willingness to focus, directly and methodically, on what we don't yet know so that we can learn how to work with ever-increasing skill.

Books of writing advice are ambivalent about the craftsman attitude. The majority of these focus on writing fiction, and fiction is considered to be a form of art, not craft. These books can imply that the writing process is imaginative alchemy, done by and for a special class of people. Even nonfiction advice books, designed to help readers produce seemingly less mysterious forms of writing—journalism, magazine articles, and essays—can fuel the unhelpful notion that writing springs from a creative process that needs only to be nurtured and then set free.

The classic argument for applying a craftsman attitude to academic life is "On Intellectual Craftsmanship" by sociologist C. Wright Mills.[1] This essay explicitly advocates treating social science scholarship as a craft. Mills encourages the reader to develop his (and, we must assume, her) own "habits of good workmanship."

Mills, an avid carpenter, details the tools of the sociological trade: carefully recorded and organized ideas, plans, references, and evidence. He describes how he keeps files of his own research problems, collects and organizes his own and others' theories and methods, and explains (with somewhat boring specificity while ignoring the significant contributions of two of his three wives) how he uses this written record to do his sociological work.

Mills also uses the essay to express his frustration with "turgid and polysyllabic" academic writing. As he puts it, "To overcome the academic prose you have first to overcome the academic pose." Academic posing is detrimental to our writing and fuels many of the myths that stand in our way. Mills believes (and I agree) that "the intellectual workman forms his own self as he works toward the perfection of his craft. . . . He constructs a character which has as its core the qualities of the good workman."

Another compelling account of the value of the craftsman attitude, for the quality both of our selves and of our academic work, is Patricia Limerick's essay "Dancing with Professors: The Trouble with Academic Prose."[2] Limerick, a historian of the American West, tells us to use carpenters and other artisans as "the emotional model for writers." Doing so, she argues, helps us think of our writing as "challenging craft, not as existential trauma."

Her takedown of professorial pretension is a must read. Limerick offers an insider's view of why academic prose is so bad, but she also

1. This essay was an appendix to his classic book *The Sociological Imagination* (New York: Oxford University Press, 1959). Mills was a motorcycle-riding Columbia University sociology professor whose other books were widely read, especially *White Collar* (New York: Oxford University Press, 1951) and *The Power Elite* (New York: Oxford University Press 1956).

2. Originally published as an essay in the *New York Times*, October 31, 1993; collected in Patricia Limerick, *Something in the Soil: Legacies and Reckonings in the Old West* (New York: W. W. Norton, 2000).

offers a devastating account of why professors are so insecure. Using Tweedledum and Tweedledee, high school dances, and the backstory of the buzzard scene in the movie *Lonesome Dove*, Limerick explains why we professors choose "camouflage and insulation over clarity and directness" in our writing. Her analysis identifies fear (of humiliation, rejection, attack) as the underlying reason for our common allegiance to "the cult of obscurity" in academic life.

Both Limerick and Mills believe that thinking of ourselves as craftspersons will help free us from becoming poseurs and thereby help us to do better intellectual work. Mills puts it in terms of character, Limerick as a way to let go of self-aggrandizing drama. The craftsman attitude lets us imagine ourselves more humbly and effectively, which helps us both think and write more effectively. More recent books by Richard Sennett[3] and Matthew B. Crawford[4] also argue that the habits and values we learn through working with our hands can and should be applied to the life of the mind.

Limerick's reference to "existential trauma" acknowledges the emotional thickets that can entangle us in academic life, especially when we run into writing trouble. Your ventilation file (detailed in the chapter 4 discussion of "taming techniques") can become a place to dump—and thereby identify—your personal array of writing-deflecting existential angst. These feelings are fueled by a puffed-up view of intellectual work. The craftsman attitude rightly drains the drama (as discussed in chapter 8), deflating our grandiose versions of what we are up to when we sit down to write.

To test this, see how well your reasons for not writing work when they are applied to building a shelf or weeding a garden. Write down all the emotional baggage that comes up when you sit down to write, then substitute "shelf" or "garden" for your writing project. See if your angst still sounds reasonable and appropriate. While surely carpenters and gardeners can also struggle with self-doubt and frustration, my guess is that we academics are far more insecure about our abilities, because we want so much to be perceived as "already" experts.

3. *The Craftsman* (New Haven, CT: Yale University Press, 2008).
4. *Shop Class as Soulcraft: An Inquiry into the Value of Work* (New York: Penguin Books, 2009).

Too often we treat our academic work as a measure of our inner worth, rather than as a process of learning how to use a specific set of skills. We hobble ourselves if we believe our writing ability is evidence of having (or not having) the "right academic stuff." Remember, your current ability to do academic writing is not really evidence of your innate intellectual abilities. It is evidence of whether you've had access to, and experience with, effective writing tools and habits. When we invoke the ivory tower or the artist's studio rather than the woodworking shop, the prospect of academic writing produces Limerick's "existential trauma" rather than Mills's DIY spirit.

When we imagine ourselves as aspirants, trying to sound smart enough to join an exclusive elite, we fall prey to all kinds of writing-deflecting drama. Aspirants agonize about their abilities and the value of their path, while craftspeople focus on learning how to do the work. The craftsman attitude helps us remember that academic writing requires methodical practice of appropriate skills. It need not be experienced as an exalted quest to "make the grade." A craftsman attitude puts the focus on performing the work, rather than performing a self.

Treating academic writing as a craft enables us to be more effective in both our writing and our thinking. It makes it more likely that we will give ourselves daily low-stress, high-reward contact with our project rather than becoming distracted, depressed, stuck, and blocked. It can restore us to "right size" when we find ourselves intimidated or arrogant. It helps us stay modest and hopeful rather than grandiose and insecure. It helps us focus on doing our project rather than on whatever good or bad outcomes we may imagine for it.

So become willing to define yourself as an academic apprentice. Dedicate yourself to practicing your craft. Keep your focus where it needs to be—on the work, not the self. In solidarity with all good craftspeople, gather effective tools (detailed in the next section) and cultivate effective habits. Patiently secure the time, space, and energy your work requires. Let a craftsman attitude help you get the job done.

Part Two

· ·

USING TOOLS THAT WORK

A writing project, especially when we don't spend time with it every day, may come to feel overwhelming. It begins to feel like a predator waiting to pounce—and who would want to show up for that? Once we lose contact with writing, we find many plausible reasons to stay away. But avoiding our writing just makes things worse. We need instead to find ways to establish safe and steady writing engagement.

The next chapter offers you three key techniques to "tame" your writing project. Then, in the chapters that follow, I describe ways to secure writing time, space, and energy. The concrete tools offered in this section help you maintain consistent and rewarding contact with your writing project.

. . . .

W hen I was having trouble writing my dissertation, I came across three simple writing techniques in David Sternberg's classic *How to Complete and Survive a Doctoral Dissertation*. They reduced my fear and allowed me to successfully complete my dissertation.

I still use these techniques with every article and book I write. Whenever I feel lost or anxious or overwhelmed, these three get me back on track. I call them "taming techniques" because they allow you to organize and connect with your project while detaching from your anxiety. They lower the stakes and show you, day after day, that it is possible to write often and happily. They are fundamental to giving yourself what you most need: frequent, low-stress encounters with your project. The three taming techniques are these:

Create a project box.
Use a ventilation file.
Write at least fifteen minutes every day.

The *project box* is a way to organize your project so that it doesn't loom over you like a dark, amorphous cloud. The project box is an organized set of files that breaks your project into smaller sections and allows you to collect and contain key elements.

I'm old school and use a portable hanging file box, available at office supply stores for under twenty dollars. It has a lid and holds labeled hanging files. I like the tangibility of paper and the process of organizing sheets of paper into specific files. But you can create an electronic "project box" dedicated to your academic writing by creating a different username in your computer system for the purpose.[1] You could also use a separate laptop just for your writing projects. The point is to have a way to open and close your project that keeps it organized, accessible, but clearly separated from your other commitments.

1. My thanks to Kristina Quynn, founder of CSU Writes!, for this suggestion.

My book project files usually include Outlines (various overviews); Questions (that I want to answer through the project); Next Steps; References; Chapter X Notes (ideas and outlines for each chapter or section); Submission Plans; To Be Added; and the absolutely essential Ventilation File (see below). But you can make whatever files you want, as long as they organize and contain all relevant elements of a particular project.

Scholarly projects expand and mutate. It is disorienting to deal with an ever-changing collection of possibilities, most of them mutually exclusive. Disorganized electronic versions of various files can daze and confuse us, offering the illusion of progress when we are actually just spinning our wheels. A box of hanging files, including outlines and questions, allows me to create structure and focus for an ever-shifting project.

I've tried to do without a project box, but I find that my writing starts to seem like an intrusive heap of loose ends and false starts. With a project box, the chaos of my intellectual work is corralled into organized sections, and those sections seem to be waiting patiently for me to return to them every time I open the lid.

This means that—for this project as well as for previous books—I have an old-fashioned box with hanging files with printed labels sitting by my desk, waiting for my visits. I don't have piles of books and articles and a laptop crowded with cryptic titles and abandoned outlines, along with half-finished drafts, all calling my name and haunting my psyche. I compose on my laptop and save written files there, but I organize my project using a real box, and it works for me.

But even when safely corralled, my project can start to feel toxic or pointless. I begin to avoid and doubt it, and so resist working on it. This is where the amazing power of the *ventilation file* comes in. This file offers me a confidential space for every hostile, resentful, negative thing that I think and feel when I try to write. The ventilation file, as described by Sternberg, has truly changed my writing life

If I have a project box organizing my writing and I am committed to opening my project box for at least fifteen minutes a day (see below), but I am still resisting writing, then something important is up. My writing problem is not about organization, and it is not about time, since I have committed myself only to writing fifteen minutes a day.

Something else is going on. If I ignore that "something else," it will just get stronger or come back in another guise.

The great thing about the ventilation file is that it acknowledges and incorporates my resistance to writing into the project itself. Rather than trying to hide from or ignore or overcome my writing issues, I can engage them directly via the ventilation file. For my fifteen minutes of project-writing a day, I get to explore why I don't want to be doing it at all.

I get to write about how boring and wrongheaded and pointless the project is, or I feel, or my life seems. After fifteen minutes of free, unexpurgated expression of whatever is coming up, I can get on with my day. I've "done my time" and am off the hook. I will revisit the project box tomorrow, and maybe I will feel a little better then.

And I almost always do. Apparently giving myself permission to express hostility toward the project (or myself or my life) opens up possibilities for me to move forward. It works—somehow—to make the project less daunting, more tame and familiar. The ventilation file is the most crucial and helpful piece of advice I have to offer you. Please try it, no matter how skeptical you are or how unnatural or self-indulgent it seems. It is an amazingly powerful writing tool.

The ventilation file gives me a way to safely engage my many, constantly mutating, mostly self-generated writing obstacles. Once I've written about all the reasons I don't want to write, I can set these reasons aside or address them through other means—therapy, talking with friends, advice from colleagues. By giving supportive space to whatever is standing in my way, the ventilation file lets me get on with my writing project.

The ventilation file is a nonjudgmental arena to express the doubts and fears that academic writing so often generates. You don't have to reread what you've written, and you can erase or tear it up if you prefer. But if you do choose to reread, you will discover what you are telling yourself about the project, your abilities, and your situation. These writing-related beliefs deserve your attention, and we deal with them in section III. The ventilation file allows you to incorporate your writing resistance into your writing process, and it gives you a way to identify and respond to the writing myths that may be standing in your way.

So the project box organizes and the ventilation file detoxifies. But what about the *fifteen minutes a day* idea? Surely no one can get a scholarly writing project finished by writing only a few minutes every day?

Well, yes, you can, if that's really all you can manage. I first heard about this technique in Virginia Valian's engaging essay "Learning to Work."[2] When Valian was beginning her academic career, fifteen minutes was the maximum amount of time she could force herself to write before she became overwhelmed by anxiety. She asked her boyfriend to time her, and she collapsed as soon as her fifteen minutes ended. But as she became able to meet her time commitment, over and over, her anxieties diminished. Eventually she learned how to connect reliably with intellectual work. She went on to have a successful academic career as a psycholinguist and writer.

Research on writing productivity confirms her experience. As Boice (in *Professors as Writers*) and others have shown, brief daily contact with a writing project results in more creativity and productivity than long intermittent writing bouts do. In other words, the binge writing (up all night, against deadline pressure) we learned to do in college doesn't work in the long run. We do not need huge swaths of time to do our writing. Instead what works best is contained, inviting "writing minutes" as often as possible.

Writing for a mere fifteen minutes every day allows us an end-run around the many psychic obstacles that can so easily deflect us. If necessary, using the ventilation file during that time allows us to express and let go of whatever may be standing in our way. I recommend planning six rather than seven writing sessions each week. This means that if you miss a day, you can just take it off guilt-free. What matters is the frequent low-stress, high-reward contact.

Obviously, once you get rolling you will want to devote more time to your academic writing. In the next section I offer multiple suggestions for ways to secure that time. But by being committed to your daily fifteen minutes, you will be able to stay productive and guilt-free, in calm daily contact with your organized project even when the

2. In *Working It Out: 23 Women Writers, Artists, Scientists, and Scholars Talk about Their Lives and Work*, ed. Sara Ruddick (New York: Pantheon, 1977).

semester is in full swing and you are drowning in other demands, or when you feel frozen by resistance and hostility.

These techniques, especially the project box, allow you to fully engage with (and fully disengage from) your writing. They allow you to stop feeling like you "ought to be writing" all the time. Without these techniques there is no easy way to turn off a writing project, and that constant anxiety drains and corrodes our writing spirits.

So that's it—three tools that let you contain, cleanse, and connect to academic writing. *Project box plus ventilation file plus fifteen minutes a day.* Are these really all you need to write productively for the rest of your life? Yes and no. Just as most diet advice is some version of "eat less, move more," most writing advice is some version of "fear less, write more."

My suggestions in this book are predicated on your willingness to apply these three taming techniques. When you find yourself fearing, loathing, and avoiding your academic writing, these techniques will get you back on track. They allow your project to feel less like a wild beast lurking in the jungle and more like a friendly pet, eager for its daily walk. They are simple, proven ways to help you to "fear less, write more." I encourage you to commit to them and see what happens.

5 } SECURING TIME

. . . .

A t the beginning of every semester, many of us schedule time for research. If we are lucky, we can carve out a particular weekday, or several mornings or afternoons that we hope to devote to scholarship. We have every intention of keeping to our schedule. But each semester our non-class time gets given away to other obligations. We agree to a department meeting or to use our writing time "just this once" to get some grading done. Our writing time fills up with all kinds of other necessary academic work. We vow that next week (or month or semester) we will really get going on our writing project—but this week, we really are swamped.

Every day we don't write becomes another day we feel frustrated and guilt-ridden. Week after week, we feel like we are being deflected from writing by outside forces. Under these conditions it is easy to succumb to self-pity, shame, or delusion. The self-pity is because we feel burdened by the legitimate demands of teaching and service and family commitments. The shame is because we believe that, busy as we are, we should nonetheless be writing for hours on end. And the delusion is that sometime very soon we will be able to write a lot—if we can just get through this week.

No matter what their discipline, career stage, or administrative position, my colleagues come to faculty writing workshops and counseling with the same "time" issue. They believe that academic writing requires big chunks of time, and this week/month/semester they don't have the four to six hours several times a week that they are sure they need to really get writing. They combine a sense that they have to meet other demands first with the belief that next week it will be easier to free up the many consecutive hours they think they need. This prevents them from securing time to write today and tomorrow, and the day after that.

What we really need to do is to *secure* writing time. We don't find time (it's always there) or make time (it's not ours to make), but we can learn how to organize and protect the hours we are given every day. I like the way "securing time" sounds—it implies the protecting of something valuable. So how, in our demanding academic schedule, can we secure time to write?

The first step is to find out where your time is actually going. Getting an accurate assessment of what is truly filling your time isn't as easy as it sounds. Most of us rush around in a blur, feeling stressed and busy but also inefficient and inadequate. We don't keep track of all the things that claim our time and attention. All we know is that our life feels like a pressured sprint. This means that "when do I have time to write?" isn't a question we can answer, because all we know for sure is that we don't have "enough" time right now.

So spend a week keeping a "reverse day planner." Instead of using a planner to record upcoming events, use one to record what you actually devote time to over the course of each day. Record when and for how long you check e-mail, prepare courses, grade papers, write letters of recommendation, meet with students and colleagues. Include routine tasks—food preparation, dishes, laundry, groceries, errands, driving, and walking the dog. Put in everything nonacademic: exercising, social media, meeting friends, watching TV, surfing the net, puttering, sleeping, and staring at the wall. Where is your time going?

After a few days of keeping a reverse day planner, I saw that I was a whirling dervish of unexamined commitments. I realized I had been trying to balance the stress of work and family with "self-care"—journaling, exercise, recreational reading, and volunteer work. I wanted a balanced life and had been adding in "counterbalance" to an already demanding schedule. My life was overstuffed, and so no wonder I was rushed, exhausted, and frustrated, and could never "find" enough time to write.

What the reverse day planner showed me was how I was currently choosing to live. It recorded my default priorities—where I was actually putting my time, every day. Whatever is filling up your days right now is what you are prioritizing. Once you look honestly at what you are giving priority to, you can ask yourself: are all of these commitments more important to me than writing?

My reverse planner showed me that I was spending my best and most energetic time on e-mail. It also showed me how many hours I was devoting to enhancing and invigorating my classes, in spite of having taught them before. It showed me that I was saying yes to service requests (departmental and community) that helped me feel like I was making a difference. The reverse day planner helped me see that I was trying to spend more time with friends and family, and doing things like yoga and meditation, to help me relax and feel better about how unbalanced my life felt. No wonder academic writing felt like one more burden to be added onto an overloaded life—it was.

When academic writing is just one more thing we feel obligated to cram into an overstuffed life, it creates resentment and resistance. We can circumvent that at first by the commitment to our prescribed fifteen minutes—because all of us can find fifteen minutes each day. But to have a productive academic writing career over many years, we need a different relationship with time. Rushing around, or choosing to "lean in" and "do it all," doesn't work when it comes to writing.

What most of us need is to be writing, happily, for an hour or two several days a week, in addition to our daily fifteen-minute check-ins. If we have an upcoming deadline we need to meet, then several hours every day is the most effective schedule. The only way we can secure that kind of time is to give writing a place of honor—to make it a true priority, not "one more commitment" in an overstuffed life. Once I saw what I was doing, I was able to secure two hours of morning writing time three to five days a week. To my surprise, everything else got done anyway. In part this was because I put off e-mail until later and didn't need to spend as much time on course preparation, and once the writing became rewarding, I didn't need as much yoga and meditation and volunteer work to help me feel better.

The reverse day planner helps us let go of the self-pity, shame, and delusion that keep us fruitlessly trying to fit writing into our academic schedule year after year. The planner showed me that I was not (as I secretly feared) too lazy, disorganized, or inefficient to write every day. I really was (thanks to my own choices) too busy to write.

This recognition—based on reality, not vague ideas about how I spent my time—allowed me to make a commitment, every day, to protect an hour or two of writing time from being invaded by busyness. It encouraged me to treat my academic writing as something important and valuable, not just one more thing to try to shoehorn in next week. It allowed me to be in charge of how I allocated at least some of my time, instead of continuing to feel like I was under siege from the demands of others. It feels tons better. And it works.

I have no idea what a reverse day planner will reveal to you, but I know it will be an eye-opener. When colleagues do this, they are stunned to see what they are unintentionally prioritizing, as well as how truly busy they really are. Once they see where their time is actually going, they can let go of self-recrimination and delusions and instead become strategic about protecting the time they need to write.

If you create an accurate record of all your activities, you will find out exactly what you are currently prioritizing, because where we spend our time is how we spend our lives. Then you will be able to decide—consciously—if these really are the priorities you want. If writing is so important to your career and to your psyche, shouldn't it come first, not last? Be willing to put your writing in a place of honor.

Design a writing plan calendar that designates specific times during the week for writing; then count the number of these you actually have per semester or summer. Use this calendar to block off travel times, grading times, and other writing disruptions so you know approximately how many writing sessions you have before a specific deadline or benchmark like the end of a semester or summer. Keep a running count. Recently a group of colleagues in a semester planning workshop found that we had fewer than thirty writing sessions each semester, once we accounted for travel and grading. In other words, we didn't have "all semester" to meet our May deadlines, just twenty-five or so brief (one- to three-hour) writing sessions.

This kind of concrete specificity makes it less easy for us to forfeit our ever-dwindling supply of writing sessions. It helps us be less willing ("just this once") to give it away. It is all too easy to fall for quasi-crises—seemingly urgent requests involving someone else's pending deadline. Many of us change our own schedules because we don't want to inconvenience or disappoint someone else. Many of us like to get small tasks "out of the way" before we turn to our project, using up most of our supposedly protected-for-writing time.

What listing regular writing hours on a writing plan calendar teaches me is that almost everything can be put aside for a few hours while I write—and nothing bad happens! The urgency I feel is almost always unnecessary. I can write regularly and grading still gets done, letters and reports get written, other meeting or appointment times end up working just fine. It feels like a radical act to refuse distractions—to close the door not just on burdensome tasks but also on pleasant distractions. But that is what we need to do in order to write.

Identify, count, and then secure your writing time each week. Close the door for a few hours and open the project box, in the midst of all your other obligations, real and perceived. Both the burdensome tasks and the pleasant distractions will wait. Your writing won't.

Recording your writing time, along with your other commitments, helps keep you from giving it away. Once you know how you are currently filling your days, you can choose to give your writing pride of place—the protected time it both needs and deserves.

6 } SECURING SPACE

. . . .

The main thing that all writers need, Stephen King says in *On Writing*, is "a door that you are willing to shut." The door (if we use it) protects us from interruptions. A space where we are protected from interruption is crucial for any writing project.

But unlike Stephen King, professors are not full-time writers. Much of our job is actually "open door"—we are expected to make ourselves available to students and colleagues as needed. It can feel hostile, as well as lonely, to lock ourselves away from others for hours at a time. This is true both at work and at home.

Campus offices are not designed for writing. We may hope to make them writing friendly by coming in early or staying late. We may put notes on our door saying we are writing so please don't disturb. But our campus offices remain open, permeable spaces for two reasons—they allow us to be legitimately interrupted by students and colleagues, and they make it easy for us to interrupt ourselves with e-mail and class preparation and departmental duties.

Our campus offices are where we plan our teaching and do our departmental work. They are physically and psychically connected to obligations that can and will distract us from our scholarship. So even if we physically close an actual office door, we may still be psychologically on call.

In my campus office I am always aware of papers that need grading, e-mail that needs answering, and recommendation letters that are coming due. It is hard for me to shift into writing mode and stay there, even at night or on weekends. It is fine for short bouts, for outlining and copyediting, but for truly productive writing I need—and strongly recommend—a separate, dedicated writing space protected from interruption.

The opposite of a campus office is a fantasy writing space. I have a history of creating home writing spaces that I never use. Whatever space I tried to set up for writing (and I really enjoyed getting it all arranged) quickly became storage for out-of-season clothes, extra furniture, and writing projects I would never get around to doing. I even bought a 1981 VW camper, thinking I would park it in the backyard and write there every day. It's a lovely idea, except it always seemed too hot or too cold or too damp or too sunny—maybe tomorrow?

For years I thought all I really needed to be a productive writer was the perfect writing space. Like most delusions, this was partly true. But what I needed wasn't my distracting campus office or a fantasy writing studio. What I needed was a door that I could close on an organized, inviting place to write, coupled with a commitment to go there every day, for at least a few minutes. I just didn't know how to give that to myself.

I envied colleagues who had spare rooms they turned into idyllic spaces that looked just like my fantasy—books neatly lining the shelves, a large desk, with lamps and comfy chairs and beautiful views. If only I had something like that, the words would just pour out! But gradually I realized that, just like me, these colleagues rarely used their writing spaces, no matter how beautifully decorated they were.

A "door that we are willing to shut" needs to protect a truly functioning space, not a pretty fantasy. We can waste a lot of time and energy yearning for, designing, creating, and then not using idyllic writing spaces, or we can give ourselves simple, inexpensive basics and actually use them.

The TU campus library has a beautiful faculty lounge set aside for us. It is ideal for reading, thinking, grading, and also for writing. The library also has small study carrels available for semester-long use. Yet surprisingly few faculty members use either of these options. Before tenure they think that they need to be seen writing—always visible in their open-door office. After tenure they just keep on trying to make their campus office work.

Many of the colleagues I've advised through the faculty writing program have set aside writing space in their homes. But they aren't inviting or usable spaces. Over time these home offices have become storage spaces, filled with writing-related debris like unfinished manuscripts, projects that have derailed, collaborations that may or may not work out. They are actually places to avoid because they have become, as one colleague put it, "a shrine to my writing failures."

So think about what the best writing space can be for you—not as a fantasy but as a simple reality that you can create and maintain with minimal effort. My colleague with the "failure shrine" took just two hours to clear out his unrelated clutter, box up old projects, and put up a whiteboard for his current project. Suddenly he was good to go—he had an organized, focused, functional writing space.

What if you don't yet have a writing space in your house? Designate one and make it work. Some options that colleagues have tried include clearing out a storage area, screening a part of an unused dining room, retrieving part of a guest room. In each case they created a usable—if not picture-perfect—uninterruptible space.

A functional writing space, used often, allows us to arrange words with minimum distraction and maximum ease. The successful academic writers I know protect their writing space with zeal. Some even rent space in an office building, or in a neighbor's home, because someone else's house is never as distracting as one's own.

For me, cafés are like the dream study—they seem like the right setting but they aren't always a productive space. Coffee shops can give the illusion that we are writing when mostly we are "looking writerly." But there are people who can be truly productive in a café, and if that is you, then go for it—just make sure that you really are "shutting the door" on all interruptions and that you have exactly what you need to move your project forward.

I believe our writing spaces should contain only what we need right now, for the project at hand. Those who believe in feng shui will tell you that old projects have stalled energy, so we should store them elsewhere. Chi or no chi, I guard against my tendency to put half-done or "someday" research in the space where I'm trying to write. Being surrounded by multiple unfinished projects is disheartening and distracting. So I'm learning how to clear, protect, and invigorate space for what I am actually working on.

Once you've secured a dedicated space and can truly shut the door to protect it, what else do you need? I like my space to be organized and feel inviting, and here's what works for me.

I am writing this in a 6×10-foot enclosed sun porch off the living room of my house. On the side facing the driveway I have a small table and chair, a desk lamp, a calendar, shelves, and a metal ironing board that I can use as a standing desk if I get tired of sitting. The ironing board also works as a space to spread out project support material, if needed. My project box is stored beside the desk. On the windowsill I have Post-it notes, pens and pencils, and a few favorite objects. Behind me I have a reading chair, a lamp, another bookshelf, and small file cabinets holding my printer. Even though the room is small and I have non–project-related things in half of the room, the table / project box / ironing board is my writing space. And yes, it has a door that closes.

But what do we do about the knocks at our digital door—interruptions through our computers or phones? I once had a laptop that had lost its wireless capacity, which made it easy to stay away from e-mail and the Internet. But there are programs that can do the same thing, if you need to prevent yourself from tempting electronic distractions. I keep my cell phone on silent and let the home phone take a message. And because I can still hear household noises through the closed door, I have earplugs or headphones to use as needed (especially useful when my children were young).

A key to keeping my space inviting is to keep it project-focused. I still struggle with my tendency to store not-sure-where-else-to-put-it stuff nearby. But I'm learning how to put completed or stalled projects or maybe-someday materials outside my door in labeled cardboard boxes. It's not pretty (a stack of cardboard storage cartons in the living room behind a screen), but it keeps my writing space project-focused.

Some people put up whiteboards that they update regularly. This keeps their project (and their progress on it) visible. The prolific social critic Lewis Mumford nailed a series of industrial clipboards over his desk. This kept sections of his project in front of him at all times. I use my project box to keep track of overviews, outlines, and sections and use a small notebook to record my writing hours. Sometimes I spread project chunks out on the ironing board. When working on big projects, we need some way to keep the forest in view as we work on the trees.

Sometimes I think I need expensive products to stay organized. This, like my writing studio fantasy, is a delusion I keep falling for. If leather accessories, color-coding, and elaborate systematizing help lower your stress, increase your reward, and foster your writing, great—high-end office supply sites like Levenger and Bindertek offer a wealth of tempting options. But if these aspirational products just help you accessorize a writing space you never use, it's time to get back to basics.

My turquoise metal ironing board has been with me since my dissertation. I bought it at a garage sale for five dollars. The desk I'm using is a 1960s-era Formica-topped table I got free from a campus storage unit. My file cabinets came from a store that sold used office supplies. The project box cost fifteen bucks. My bookshelves are adjustable fiberboard—the kind that eventually warp but will last for ten to twenty years.

Obviously, I didn't have to buy the VW or dream of renting a separate studio or envy someone else's perfectly appointed space. I didn't have to imagine renovating this sun porch with new flooring and built-in shelves and a lovely expandable corner desk (I actually priced and saved for this option for several years). All I ever really needed was a desk, a chair, and a project box. It took me a very long time to figure that out.

So give your scholarly work the dedicated, inviting, and orderly writing space it deserves. Don't fall for the delusion that you need to be visible to your colleagues and available to your students 24/7 or that you need the perfect writing studio. Don't assume that the junk-filled place you think you should be using is good enough as is. If your campus office isn't working (and it probably isn't!), try out other options. Find a quiet spot in the library, or clear and organize space at home, or rent a room in your neighborhood.

If you are constantly designing but not really using fantasy writing studios, let go of the dream. Create a simple, serviceable space, close the door, and open your project box.

. . . .

Protecting writing energy is key to academic productivity, but very few of us have learned how to work with—rather than just use up—our creative powers. Energy fluctuates every day, in relation to what we are doing with our minds and bodies. Most of us pour out energy until we are exhausted, and then keep going anyway. We treat our energy as a necessary but limited resource, because that is how we've experienced it.

I think, instead, we should treat our energy as a reliable, renewable resource. We can learn how to use writing to energize us for other aspects of our life. Rather than turning our writing into "one more thing" that burdens and drains us, we can make it into a source of energy. That is how we learn to work with our energy rather than just using it up.

We need to respect our energy patterns if we want to be productive academic writers. Yes, it is important to use basic techniques to connect effectively with our project, and we need to find ways to secure frequent low-stress, high-reward writing times. And it helps us to have an inviting, orderly writing space with "a door that we are willing to shut." But once we have tamed our project and secured the writing time and the space we need for it, we still need to learn how to work with our own writing energy if we are truly to support our scholarship.

In his academic writing advice book, *The Clockwork Muse*, Eviatar Zerubavel says, "Just as you optimize your other writing conditions, learn to identify the best times for your writing" (21). He suggests you keep track of when you feel most and least productive in the course of a week, and then use this knowledge to identify your best hours for writing. What he is offering is a way to match your writing time to your writing energy.

Call your most energetic hours A time. Your goal is to protect your A time from all the B and C tasks that tend to fill it up. B tasks require alertness and focus, but not necessarily your best creative energy. C tasks are mostly rote—work that doesn't require as much insight or creativity as writing does. Start valuing yourself enough to assign A time to A tasks, B time to B tasks, and C time to C tasks.

Recently a colleague told me she doesn't really understand this ABC stuff. She just goes flat out every day and then collapses. She does the same the next day, and the day after. She is a dedicated professor in the midst of writing yet another book, does more than her share of university service, and has two young children. Her strategy was mine for many years: pour energy into everything and hope that a decent night's sleep will help me survive the demands of the next day.

The problem with this strategy, from a writing perspective, is that it is undifferentiated: everything gets whatever energy we have at the moment that we encounter it. We deal as best we can with what is in front of us, forcing ourselves to generate enough energy for all the tasks in our day, over and over. Exhaustion becomes constant, as does frustration, even resentment, as we keep trying to generate the energy we need for all that is on our schedule.

I've come to recognize this, in myself, as a siege mentality. I feel as if I am being bombarded by unwelcome demands, most of which I do not want to meet, or cannot possibly meet, or could meet, sort of, if someone else (grrrr!) would just do their undone part. I have become a victim, and nothing drains energy faster than feeling trapped and powerless.

This work-until-you-drop pattern keeps us from recognizing that what our academic responsibilities require of us actually varies. It keeps us from making and honoring our own choices. We can—we must—recognize and respect our fluctuating energies. We need to learn how to match energy to task—put A energy into A tasks, B energy into B tasks, and C energy into C tasks.

We are not horses straining to pull carts loaded with other people's needs and demands. We get to decide how and when to load our own cart, each and every day. We are neither trapped nor powerless. We don't have to keep pulling every burden as hard as we can until the day is done. We can match our energies to our priorities. We can figure out when we are at our energetic best—most alert and creative—and match that time to an important commitment: our scholarly writing.

I have another colleague who resisted the ABC method because he felt that it relegated his students, family, and friends to some lesser status, as if he were giving them a C or B rather than an A. But this method is not a grading scheme—or an evaluation of essential worth. It is a way to let different elements of our life feed us in different ways. When my creative energy is drained, I can be refueled by time with family or a walk with a friend. If I am matching energy to task, then a good classroom discussion or a productive faculty meeting can re-energize me. A swim or a yoga class can be timed to revive me, rather than just be scheduled as another must-do.

This ABC matching system allows me to take into account the different kinds of energy that different elements of my life both use and offer. It is a calibrated exchange system that allows me to take full advantage of what gives as well as takes different kinds of energy. It keeps me from feeling like a marionette, dancing to everyone else's tunes.

Scholarship is our primary requirement for academic success, yet it is also the easiest of our responsibilities to put off. There is a time-management technique that asks us to arrange our responsibilities into a four-by-four quadrant according to their urgency and importance. Academic writing is a classic example of a non-urgent but important task, the kind that usually gets pushed aside, because our days are always full of things that seem to need our immediate attention, some important, some not.

Until we learn to focus on what matters most and then match our energy to tasks, we will let urgency determine what gets first dibs, even if the task is not all that important. We squander our energies on immediate and seemingly urgent e-mails, memos, and meetings just to get them "out of the way," thereby lowering our anxiety and making us feel like we're accomplishing something. Our scholarship keeps getting pushed to the back burner.

When our scholarly writing gets deflected, it leads to daily frustration that only increases our anxiety. Frustration and anxiety are inherently exhausting, so they combine to drain our energies *and* deflect our writing. We try to "get back" to our project, but it keeps getting delayed by whatever urgent B and C tasks are calling to us. Until we find ways to appropriately match tasks to energies, we stay stuck in workhorse mode, growing ever more burdened and exhausted.

So pay attention to how energy works in your life. What gives you energy? What drains you? What are your daily energy patterns? You can explore this with your reverse day planner. When do you feel most focused and alert—morning, or evening, or midday? How do you feel after exercise or a meal or a nap? Do you leave the classroom exhilarated or exhausted—and how can you respond to that skillfully? How do you feel after a department meeting? A committee meeting? Fifteen minutes of writing? An hour? Three hours? Analyze your energy patterns by trying (as Zerubavel suggests) daily energy tracking. What energizes you, and when do you have what it takes to do your very best work?

Our scholarly work deserves A energy. Writing and revising require intense creative attention—we need to be "all there," at our very best. The focused, active, engaged mental energy that writing requires is also needed for research, but not always and not for all elements of it. Consider which parts of your research process require A energy—things like designing new projects, planning grant proposals, and organizing lab priorities. Other aspects of our work, including designing new courses, may also require A energy.

But routine coursework, like preparation for a class we have taught before, usually requires B energy. We can and should give our classes clear focus and attention, but they need not sap all of our precious A energy. E-mail, grading, advising, reports, and faculty meetings are mostly C-level tasks—they can be done responsibly even when we aren't at our creative best. Much as at tenure time, research, teaching, and service are in descending order of creative energy allocation. Not in terms of ultimate value, but in relation to the level of intense focus they require.

I have come to see how my energy is renewable during the day—and this is making a profound difference in how I approach my work. Most of my life I've believed my energy is a scarce resource that is being drained by too many demands. My only coping strategies were to try to say no more frequently, try to get more exercise and sleep, and hope I'd feel better in a few days. I spent far too many years resenting the many time-consuming demands of teaching and service, rather than figuring out how to let them become sources of energy.

My most creative time is early morning, and I've always known that is when I should write. But for years I would find myself doing B-level course preparation and C-level e-mails during my A time. This was because urgency—as indicated by my anxiety levels—determined my priorities. I feared being unprepared and letting people down, so I let lecture preparations, grading, and e-mails leak into my A time "just this week" and therefore (my reverse day planner revealed) most of the semester.

The same thing still happens with time-sensitive tasks like committee reports and letters of recommendation. These feel crucial and are indeed important, but they are basically B or C tasks, so they really shouldn't get my A energy. It requires constant effort for me to remember this, because it can feel so good to get things "off my desk."

E-mail is a seductive energy sinkhole for me. I fight the urge to check my e-mail in the morning to see if there are any fires I need to put out. A quick look (just in case) may reduce my immediate anxiety, but any contact with e-mail distracts, depresses, and drains me. I am learning to wait until my early-morning writing is done, and my classes are mostly prepared, before I jump into whatever I'm being asked to do via e-mail. I'm finally learning that almost all e-mail requests can wait a few hours and that I have the right to match my tasks to my energies.

Each of us can find ways to recognize, and work skillfully with, the stuff that drains us. Many aspects of academic life are energy vampires. Office politics, interpersonal tensions, and unwise service commitments can take a serious toll, especially when we take them—and ourselves—too seriously. Avoid energy drains as much as you can; at most, give them your C energy. As you respect your right to allocate your own attention, you will find ways to detach from aspects of academic life that truly exhaust you.

This ABC energy system gives you permission to direct energy to the academic responsibilities that really matter—the ones that give you a sense of worth and accomplishment. Giving everything that comes your way equal energy until you drop doesn't work—in service, in teaching, or in research. It sucks the joy from teaching and service as well as scholarship. But once we learn to match task to energy, we give ourselves the chance to experience what is rewarding in all facets of our professional lives.

So what actually happens to those B and C tasks when you give A energy to your scholarship every day? The reverse day planner shows me that I still get them done. I have proved to myself that I can meet my obligations even when (sometimes especially when) I use my A time for writing. The reverse day planner also shows me what happens when "just this once" I decide to check e-mail or grade or work on my lecture instead of write. I see that I have wasted yet another chance to do my best work. I deflect my scholarship and add frustration, anxiety, and guilt to my life.

Figure out how your own energy works and then allocate it appropriately. Yes, you have lots of commitments in your professional and personal life, but what they require of you really does vary. And you vary in what you can bring to every encounter. Respect yourself enough to learn how to receive as well as give energy. Then devote your best energies to what matters most.

Part Three

. . . .

CHALLENGING WRITING MYTHS

Accepting that academic life is not writing-supportive, adopting a craftsman attitude, using the three taming techniques (project box; ventilation file; at least fifteen minutes a day), and securing time, space, and energy for your writing make it possible for you to write happily and often. They are fundamental tools for writing productivity.

But encountering obstacles is an inescapable part of the writing process. Even when using these basic tools, you may still find yourself struggling, at least at times—stalled, disheartened, and deflected. The following chapters presume that you are using these effective writing tools but are encountering additional obstacles in the writing process.

This section focuses on how the writing-related stories we tell ourselves stand in our way. It asks you to recognize and challenge the myths that can keep you from frequent low-stress, high-reward encounters with a writing project you enjoy.

8 } DRAINING THE DRAMA

. . . .

I've fallen for many different dramatic narratives in my academic career. Self-created narratives about what might happen to me, or a colleague, or my department, or "the field" get me all worked up, ready to fight the good fight on the side of Truth, Justice, and Academic Excellence. Such stories get me so wound up that I can't think clearly about what might really be going on or calmly figure out what might be the right thing for me to do in response.

Under the spell of such stories, I find many seemingly good reasons not to sit at my desk every day patiently working with words, or dealing effectively with why the words aren't working. I forget all about the craftsman attitude, taming techniques, and securing time, space, and energy. I throw myself into committee work and departmental dramas, while trying to quell resentful thoughts about how I'll never get back to my writing because *they* won't let me. This can continue until I remember that I've forgotten my basic commitment: to sit down and write, even for just a few minutes, every day.

There is a famous Zen tale about what happens when we think we see a poisonous snake. We go into a panic—our heart races, and our body floods with fear. Then we realize it's just a coil of rope, not a cobra. Our panic evaporates.

The craft of academic writing is mostly rope. But when we have problems—with writing or with life—it can feel like a snake. We use way too much energy in the grip of (or trying to suppress) fear-fueled stories about how and why we can't write, and what that will mean for us and for our future. We need, instead, to learn how to recognize and work with the ordinary rope of writing.

You are caught in drama when you interpret your garden-variety writing struggles as evidence of something terribly wrong with your abilities or your situation. It is easy to start believing that fallow periods mean you will never write again, or that daily struggles are evidence of your inadequacies as a scholar, or that the demands of your situation are malign forces that make it impossible to write.

Even if you are writing and submitting effectively, you can still dramatize the publication process. You can interpret both comments and lack of comments from your colleagues or editor as signs that you are about to fail. You can interpret requests for revision as evidence that you don't know what you're doing. Yet negative feedback and editing advice are all to be expected—they are normal (often essential) elements of the writing process.

Departmental politics, the job market, and ongoing crises in higher education, as well as the overall state of the modern world and the planet, can generate drama, too. They offer us tantalizing distractions from our mundane commitment to sit down every day and find ways to write up our scholarly work. But here's the secret: keeping our daily commitment to writing gets us out of this self-generated drama. It shows us, again and again, that we are dealing with ropes, not snakes.

Because most of us hide our writing struggles, we don't let others help us keep things in perspective. Alone with our dark thoughts, our fears deepen, and we swirl in a stew of self-doubt. Have we chosen the wrong project? Are we really cut out for academic life? The longer our writing stalls, the more the drama in our head takes us over: Academe is empty, pointless, and full of mediocre phonies! It is soul-destroying! Why should we have to jump through these stupid, meaningless hoops?

This is how we turn ropes into snakes all by ourselves. Once we find ways to recognize and work skillfully with these kinds of thoughts, we drain the drama and can get back to writing a little bit every day.

Drama creation isn't easy to give up. Turning our lives into Big Deals helps us feel like we really matter because we are up to something extra-special. And academic culture is itself pretty grandiose, fueled by stories about how we can or should be making transformative contributions to our fields. As discussed in the chapter on craftsmanship, we in academe don't like to think of ourselves as humble apprentices, learning how to practice our craft.

In this section I am asking you to learn how to recognize and let go of your writing delusions so that you can write every day, either on your project or in your ventilation file. Academic writing is really a coil of rope, even when it seems like a poisonous snake.

9 } DEMONS IN FOR TEA

Writing resistance can appear anytime, even when we are deploying effective writing strategies on a project we care about. Resistance is activated, I believe, by our misguided writing myths: unconscious, self-perpetuating assumptions about who we are and what our writing should be. These myths can keep us miserable, ineffective, and stalled.

As a child, a friend of mine misheard the phrase "taken for granted" as "taken for granite." Myths about writing seem engraved in stone until we recognize and address them. They can be activated at various junctures in the writing process—when we choose a focus, apply for grants, gather our data, create a first draft, revise, and especially when we get ready to submit or resubmit. Each of these writing moments can spark debilitating writing myths.

Your ventilation file should be filling up with the debris that such myths generate. One of the best ways to identify a writing myth is to listen to what it is telling you. My myths tell me that the project is stupid, that I'll never get it done because I am on the wrong track, and besides I don't have what it takes to complete it, and even if I do get it done no one will notice or care, or if they do notice they will attack and humiliate me. These are the kinds of thoughts and feelings that writing myths support. The best way to deal with them is to figure out what, exactly, you are "taking for granite."

The myths I see most frequently—in myself and in my colleagues—are the magnum opus myth (my work must be magnificent), the hostile reader myth (and able to withstand every possible criticism), the impostor myth (but it might reveal me to be a fraud), and the compared-to-X myth (because I am not measuring up). There are related myths about the writing process, like the cleared-deck dream (writing will be easy when my current distractions disappear), the perfect first sentence (once I'm sure where to start, the rest will follow), and the need for one more source (but first I'd better make sure

I've read all relevant research). All these will be taken up in the coming chapters.

Recently I talked with a friend who was struggling with writing a thesis for her much-admired mentor. When I asked her why she was having trouble, she tried various explanations related to not having enough time or maybe having the wrong focus. Then she stopped, and her eyes filled with tears. "It's worthiness," she said softly. "I don't feel I'm worthy of writing this for her."

In that moment, my friend was letting go of her excuses—her cover story—and recognizing what was really going on. Myths show up as seemingly acceptable justifications for not getting our writing done. We keep claiming that we can't find the time, or the space, or the energy, to write. But if we can't even organize our project and spend a few minutes a day with it, then our ventilation file should be telling us why. Writing myths are misrecognitions and offer ineffective ways to address our deepest fears and feelings. Your ventilation file should be full of clues, if it is an honest record of the stories you are telling yourself about your project and process.

Writing myths manifest as muffled feelings we can't quite overcome. We ignore them, hide from them, and try to bully them into leaving us alone. But as long as the myths that feed our feelings remain etched in stone, we stay stuck. My struggling colleague was in the grip of the impostor myth and the magnum opus myth, which were ineffective attempts to deal with her feelings of unworthiness. That feeling (initially rationalized as not enough time and not the right focus) was keeping her from doing a project she has the ability and motivation to do. So now what?

I don't believe she should just "get her butt in the chair" as she was telling herself to do. Stalled writers can be incredibly self-hating, saying things like "I'm lazy. I just don't have any discipline. I need to lash myself to my desk. I need to spend every weekend locked in my office writing." This kind of harsh self-talk just feeds writing resistance.

But I don't think she should start pumping herself up with supportive slogans, either. Telling yourself you are good, kind, worthy, along with the requisite Post-it notes on the mirror and a bubble bath, can't counteract your deepest fears and feelings. Neither coercion nor affirmations are an effective antidote to deeply held myths. My friend didn't need those, nor years of therapy, in order to write her thesis. What she needed was to listen to and learn from what she was telling herself, then decide whether she should believe it.

There is a Buddhist story about the futility of trying to overpower whatever is bedeviling us. The monk Milarepa is trapped in a cave with demons, and he tries various tactics to defend against them, to no avail. Then he remembers to open his heart, become curious, and invite his demons in to talk with him over tea. They suddenly disappear. In other words, our writing demons stop deflecting our writing when we find ways to *converse with them* rather than try to ignore or fight against them.

That is what I recommended to my unworthy-feeling colleague and what I am suggesting for you. Our writing issues aren't always about the practicalities of time, space, and energy, even if we like to believe that they are. This is especially true if we find that we are resisting writing while consistently using recommended writing tools.

There are a number of books that may help you identify deeply held beliefs that could be standing in your way, including Roseanne Bane, *Around the Writer's Block: Using Brain Science to Solve Writer's Resistance*; Victoria Nelson, *On Writer's Block: A New Approach to Creativity*; and Jane Anne Staw, *Unstuck: A Supportive and Practical Guide to Working Through Writer's Block*.

If you are working on a project you care about but are unable to move forward with short, frequent writing sessions, invite your demons in for tea. Identify (without hostility or criticism) what you are telling yourself. What belief about academic writing are you "taking for granite"? Is that belief really true? If it is, and it is painful, then what can you do to support yourself? If it is not, what is more accurate, and therefore more reasonable, to believe?

The process is gentle. You are learning to stop fighting, avoiding, and denying, so that you can stop wasting energy resisting. Instead, become curious. What are your demons nattering on about now? Give them a fair hearing. If they have something true or useful to say, take them seriously. But if they are telling you myths that just stand in your way, you really don't have to listen to them anymore. Compassionate exploration is far more effective than chaining ourselves to our desk, or bucking ourselves up with slogans, or pretending we're fine when we really are not.

Writing triggers ambivalence, fear, and uncertainty in even the most successful scholars. We waste energy trying to evade unwelcome feelings based in our unexamined writing myths. We can keep pretending that all is well or keep trying to overpower our writing demons through sheer force of will. But these strategies don't work for long. Instead, figure out which writing myths you are falling for. See if you can figure out which demons are bedeviling you, and then invite them in for a chat.

· ·

The most common and damaging writing myth in academic life is that we have to create an influential masterpiece—a magnum opus. It keeps us yearning to generate an impossibly magnificent work while feeling shame for not actually doing so. This can send us into a corrosive spiral of frustration and self-hate, a spiral that makes productive writing extremely difficult. Under the influence of this myth, we find ways to avoid the writing project that is proving to us (and will therefore show the world) that we aren't as good as we think we need to be.

My first experience with the magnum opus myth was my dissertation. I wanted to write a brilliant work not just to justify my many years in school but also to live up to the "promise" that professors kept claiming they saw in me. I also needed to justify how long it was taking, given my increasing number of (semi-hidden) false starts and stalls. But the more I tried to force myself to write, the more stuck I became. The longer I was stuck, the more amazing I felt my dissertation had to be.

Finally, miserable and hoping for inspiration, I thought I'd look over the dissertations of a few of my predecessors, just to see what they had done. They were housed on a large metal shelf in the basement of the Communication library, along with the dissertations of some of my most admired professors, including my dauntingly brilliant advisor. To my surprise, the manuscripts were not surrounded by light, emanating a majestic hum. They were just sitting there, tossed in heaps, consigned to what felt like a dissertation graveyard. Each of them was well written and competent and had allowed its author to get a PhD and go on with his or her career.

Suddenly I understood that dissertations needed to be interesting, effective, professional-quality manuscripts, not transcendent masterpieces. My job was to add my own competent effort to that pile. In a few years I was able to do so, not with a field-transforming work of unmatched brilliance but with a field-contributing effort that allowed me to complete my degree, get my first job, and go on to become a productive scholar.

Some of us struggle for years with the contrast between our dreams of intellectual glory and the inadequacies of our current efforts. We can try pumping ourselves up with affirmations: "You're good enough! You're smart enough! And darn it, you *can* do great work!" We can beat ourselves up with humiliating critique: "Who do you think you are?" "This is garbage!" "Give up now!" What the dissertation shelf helped me realize is that my job was not to write something that would prove my worth or change the world, but instead to write something that could sit on that shelf alongside the best efforts of my peers.

So when you find yourself in the grip of the magnum opus myth, step back and reconsider. Does everything you write really need to change the world? Are you trying to justify your many years in graduate school, or show that you deserve to be where you are, or to be somewhere else? Do you feel obligated to do amazing work thanks to a sabbatical or fellowship? Do you still think you need to prove to your parents / high school teachers / professors that they were right (or wrong!) about you by using this writing to "become a star"? Or do you just need to write something that clarifies some ideas and contributes to your field?

Chances are good that you have the skills and ability to do valuable scholarly work. But the magnum opus myth misleads all of us into believing that competence is not enough, that our project needs to be the most influential or impressive work in the field, now and forevermore. This is not true or useful to believe. Better to think of our work as our current contribution to an ongoing conversation.

My dissertation advisor, James W. Carey, actually did change the field of media studies. Yet he himself struggled with writer's block, based in (I believe) his own version of the magnum opus myth. For years his students waited in vain for him to write a definitive, field-changing book, and he had book contracts for several possibilities. But in the end he was influential not through writing any single magnum opus but through a series of innovative essays that were eventually (through the concerted efforts of others) turned into books.

His operating metaphor was "conversation." In his introductory lecture to undergraduates, he described our common culture as a conversation that started long before we were born. We learn how we can contribute to it, buoyed by the knowledge that the conversation will continue long after we die. Our job, he told his students, is to learn from those who have gone before and make our own best contributions while we can, in support of those who come after us.

This conversation perspective offers me an antidote to the magnum opus myth, even if it couldn't do the same for him. I can commit myself to making the best contribution I can under these current and particular circumstances. This perspective is much more writing-enabling than imagining that my current project must be a masterpiece while warding off the humiliating recognition that it is not.

Instead of staying trapped by the magnum opus myth, we can learn to think of ourselves as making our best contribution to an ongoing conversation that includes insights from the past and will (we hope) incorporate at least some of our own ideas long after we are gone. We choose to build on what has gone before, and work toward helping those that come after us, by doing our best work right now.

Notice how collaborative this perspective is. The magnum opus myth, unfortunately, is both individualistic and martial: we think we must singlehandedly create work so influential that it will outshine, even obliterate, everyone else's. Our work must be so awesome that no one can ever ignore or surpass or make fun of it. Creating a magnum opus seems like a way to avoid criticism by achieving perfection—which generates even more writing demons that deflect us from doing solid work. The magnum opus myth supports grandiose fantasies while preventing modest but worthwhile success.

We need to let go of this unwinnable dialectic between dreams of glory and fears of inadequacy. Because we rightly aspire to excellence, it is hard to accept that much of what we do will be as good as we can make it but *not* the greatest that ever was. Our current project need not be so magnificent as to awe colleagues and transform the discipline. But it can and should be more than just "a ticket out of here" or a "hoop to jump through."

I see the damaging results of the magnum opus myth throughout academe. One way it manifests is in the ways that colleagues dismiss and deprecate their own scholarly efforts. Because their actual work doesn't measure up to their unrealistic yearnings, they treat it cynically. This embitters them and weakens their scholarship. Instead of finding a realistic middle path between inadequacy fears and dreams of glory, they decide to just "crank it out." They become estranged from a commitment to do their best scholarly work. One way to avoid feeling humiliated by the distance between secret dreams and actual abilities is to give up. These colleagues claim to write only because they have to "play the game"; this is the (tragic) way they justify their failure to match their own exalted expectations.

Another corrosive consequence of the magnum opus myth is what can be called colleague-contempt. In order to feel better about their own efforts, magnum opus–afflicted colleagues deprecate the work of others to prove that no one else is creating masterpieces either. They make it their job to show just how flawed everyone else's work is (while deflecting attention from their own inadequate-seeming efforts). They are cutting others down to size so that they can feel a little bit bigger—like the slightly taller mayor of Tiny Town. This kind of snide criticism of others doesn't help them get their own writing done, and it poisons the atmosphere of their department, college, university, and field.

Productive scholars don't disrespect their own work, and they don't waste their time in chronic diminishment of the work of others. In my experience, contemptuous colleagues are embittered idealists—they project onto others the gap between what they want their own scholarly work to be and what it actually is. They become cynical and unproductive, sometimes for the whole of their academic careers.

Acknowledging our own dreams of glory, and our feelings of humiliation, cynicism, contempt, and self-doubt, unravels the impasse that the magnum opus myth generates. Inviting these demons in for tea can help them disappear. This gives us a way to move forward with our work while avoiding the cynicism that offers such an ineffective resolution of it.

Recognizing the magnum opus myth also helps us appreciate its value. It is admirable to seek to do good work and to want to have an impact on our chosen field. It is understandable to feel frustrated and embarrassed by our own efforts—our reach should exceed our grasp. These understandable feelings become obstacles only when we let the magnum opus myth—rather than a desire to do our best work—motivate us. In the grip of the magnum opus myth, we become both too grandiose and too humiliated to actually write. This embitters us and keeps us from being able to make our own particular contribution to our field.

A craftsman ethic offers an antidote to the magnum opus myth. Our contribution to the larger disciplinary conversation should be as good as we can make it right now, with the tools and skills that we currently have. There will be more to come, not just from us but also from those around us. We are joining a conversation that began long ago, and we can respect what has already been thought and said and add our own voice to it. We can and should hope that our voice will make a difference and be of some service to others in years to come.

Our writing project is a moment, not a monument. It can make our corner of the discipline more accurate, insightful, or interesting. Daily contact with our writing project is evidence of our honorable intention to enhance (not transform) the scholarly conversation.

11 } THE IMPOSTOR SYNDROME

The magnum opus myth sparks a related myth: that up until now we have somehow fooled everyone about our actual abilities. This is called the impostor syndrome. Others may think we are qualified to be a successful scholar, but our current writing project will be what finally blows our cover. It will reveal us to be the unqualified, clumsy, inadequate outsider we secretly fear that we are.

Becoming a scholar means joining a guild whose primary "work" is constant evaluation. We are always grading and being graded, not just as students but also as faculty. Our publication record is the main way to prove that we measure up. It takes a tremendous amount of energy to look like we belong in the guild, always and in every way. A lifetime of trying to prove our worth can train us to hide our flaws and put on a performance. "Act like you know what you're doing. Never let them see you sweat."

You may hope that this chronic sense of having to hide your every inadequacy will disappear on its own. Maybe once you get your PhD or make it through the tenure process, you'll stop running scared. But at least in my experience, it sticks around. You can feel like a fraud even when you have an endowed chair and your vitae is a mile long. The impostor syndrome is a myth because it is not about how much you have actually done—it is about how inadequate you feel in spite of how much you have accomplished. The syndrome involves doing all you can to hide that feeling of inadequacy from others.

One way to handle the syndrome is to pretend that everything is absolutely fine. That was what I did when I was a graduate student, even as I struggled with depression, anxiety, an increasingly messy personal life, and growing doubts about academe. But I hid it all as best I could. My public face was as confident and agreeable as I could make it. I pasted on a smile and learned how to act like all was going well. No wonder I felt like a fraud.

Acting like a jerk is another strategy academics use to hide feeling of inadequacy. I've had colleagues who live their lives in attack mode—relentlessly criticizing students, their department, administrators, and each other. They attack, I presume, to feel a few moments' superiority and thus relief. They deal with their own impostor fears by heaping scorn on others.

One thing we can't do if we feel like impostors is write productively. Writing is a form of self-exposure; it makes us available for scrutiny, criticism, and evaluation. Since our writing feels like a measure of our "selves," we become paralyzed by the perceived gap between who we fear we really are and who we think we need to appear to be. Writing might reveal our fraudulence.

The impostor syndrome traps us in a self-doubting spotlight. Is what we are doing—in the lab, in the library, in the field—really any good? Rather than finding ways to do a project as well as we can, we focus (consciously or unconsciously) on keeping ourselves looking good to others. Since it will feel awful to be exposed as inadequate, maybe we should (instead of writing) attack others' work, or refuse to be edited, or browbeat students with impossible demands.

Productive writing involves an ability to focus on our project rather than ourselves. It requires that we focus on what needs to be said, rather than on the image we want to project or the effect we want to have. So in order to be productive writers, we need to find ways to invite the demon of perceived fraudulence in for tea—what can it tell us?

The impostor syndrome can be seen as evidence of our commitment to academic ideals. We feel like frauds because we want so much to be better than we are. Our fears of being "found out" are evidence of how much we want to be part of the academic community. Doing good work, in the company of colleagues we respect, is an admirable desire.

So it is not shameful to feel inadequate. It is normal, widespread, and connected to our yearning to be the kind of academic who earns respect. Intelligent, capable, and ambitious people are drawn to academe. We appreciate quality scholarship. We are ambitious enough to aspire to do very good work ourselves. And we are committed to training ourselves to do quality academic work in ways that (we hope) will deserve the respect of our peers.

But the impostor myth tells us something further. It tells us that we aren't there yet—we are still on the outside, looking in, noses pressed to the glass. We feel, at least some days, like klutzes and parvenus, also-rans who can only pretend to be the Real Deal. "They" always have it all together, and we do not. This is the classic comparison between someone else's outsides (what they seem to be) and our own insides (how we actually feel).

Facing this myth directly isn't easy. Few of us are willing to make ourselves even more vulnerable by admitting to ourselves, as well as to others, how often we feel like impostors. But letting down that facade—with ourselves and selected others—can and will lessen our fear of being exposed. I don't expect academic culture to suddenly value personal vulnerability (that will be the day!), but we can still seek the support of empathetic colleagues when we are feeling like impostors. Being honest helps destigmatize the fear that we are not measuring up. Finding out that even our most successful colleagues experience self-doubt can be incredibly liberating.

Accepting your intermittent feelings of fraudulence makes it easier to shift the spotlight back to where it belongs—on your writing project. Remember that academic writing is about making a contribution, not about proving your worth. Breaking the presumed connection between the quality of your project and your value as a person helps to dissolve the emotional energy that feeds the impostor syndrome.

This shift is a way to make yourself (not just your project) "write-sized." Just as the magnum opus myth makes the project grandiose, the impostor myth makes *us* grandiose. In its grip we are, as the saying goes, "egomaniacs with an inferiority complex." The more we imagine that writing is all about us—our skills and insights—the less competent and capable we will feel. But if we focus instead on just doing the project, and on mastering the skills we need to do it well, the more write-sized the project becomes.

It takes courage to put our research projects "out there" for evaluation. It is painful when our work doesn't measure up, whether in our own mind or in the judgment of others. But we can acknowledge our fears and move forward anyway. We can find ways to befriend feelings of inadequacy, understanding them as signs of our commitment to doing good work. We can remember that writing is about the work, not us. We are always apprentices, learning how to do better and better work. We are impostors only if we pretend otherwise.

12 } THE CLEARED-DECK FANTASY

"Clearing the decks" is the mistaken belief that we should take care of all our other obligations before we can really get going on our writing. It is one of the most widespread and damaging myths in academe.

In a recent faculty writing workshop, six colleagues committed to trying the three taming techniques on their own stalled project. They each agreed to organize a project box and write fifteen minutes a day, either on their project or in a ventilation file. We would meet in a week to explore what happened and decide on next steps.

The day before our second meeting, we all got an e-mail from T. explaining that she couldn't attend our meeting and that she hadn't been able to use any of the techniques. There was just too much going on right now, it hadn't been an opportune week for writing, and now grading had to take precedence over this week's meeting. She would be out of town the following week, but she hoped she could continue with the group once things settled down, because she definitely wanted to get back to her long-deflected project.

Obviously the "cleared-deck" fantasy (among other issues) had T. in its grip—and alas, it still does. She told us she wanted and needed to write her next book. She had been confident she could find fifteen minutes a day for it. Our workshop was right before spring break, so she had a full week ahead of her without classes. Yet she still believed there was too much else she had to do instead, before even trying the three taming techniques on her stalled book project.

We had discussed A, B, and C time in our first meeting, so she knew that brief writing contact could and should come before things like grading. She knew that frequent low-stress contact with a writing project is the secret to long-term productivity. In spite of all the information and suggestions she was given—and a supportive group of colleagues—she was not able to manage even fifteen minutes a day connecting with her book over spring break. She believed—really believed—she needed to wait to write until "things cleared up."

The rest of the group did not succumb to this fantasy. They too had other things that they needed to do. They too believed this wasn't the best week to be writing. They saw how often they were tempted, each day, to put off even a fifteen-minute commitment. But they did not—the five others were able to use the techniques, which allowed them to reconnect with their stalled projects and move forward. Once they experienced even a little progress, they felt so much relief—stalled projects drain a tremendous amount of energy. The taming techniques allowed them to feel better about their projects and about themselves, and therefore to make better choices about their next steps.

Other members of the workshop now meet regularly as a productive writing group. But our deck-clearing colleague has not rejoined them. For months she was invited, and is still on the e-mail list, but she has remained "too busy" to spend time on the book project that she said she both wanted and needed to complete. Obviously there is something deeper going on. But she won't be able to address it until she lets go of her cover story—that she has to clear the decks before she has time to write.

The point is that *things never clear up*. They don't even reliably settle down. Our inbox is always full. Our decks are always crowded. There is always more going on than we want or expect. In spite of this, we can find ways to honor our writing by putting it first and making sure it gets time and attention. Otherwise, everything *but* our writing will get done. Some days will be more crowded and demanding than others, but all the nonwriting stuff that clamors for our attention will be taken care of. Even when—I think especially when—we devote brief, frequent time to our writing.

Your reverse day planner tells how you are choosing to spend your time. As you know, it showed me that I was spending my best time on e-mail and course preparation. Most of us have jam-packed lives, and it is never easy to find long periods of uninterrupted time to write. We don't need big blocks of time, but we do need regular, brief writing sessions. Every day, not "when things settle down."

So why is protecting brief daily writing time so hard? Partly it's the misleading academic schedule, with its illusory free time "later"—on weekends, or between semesters, or in the summer. We truly believe that then we will have the time that we can't possibly spare right now.

The reality is that while we may feel less pressure when classes and committees are not in full swing, our decks will still be piled high with all the stuff we've delayed, like time with the family, relaxation, and home maintenance.

Another reason it's hard to see through this fantasy is that being "too busy" is an acceptable way to avoid the uncomfortable feelings that always accompany writing projects. I'm sure that's what is going on with T., our "too much on my plate right now" colleague. She has unacknowledged emotional baggage attached to her project, and busyness gives her a way to avoid confronting it directly. But her avoidance comes at a tremendous cost.

The longer we are away from a project, the worse we feel and the harder it is for us to reconnect with it. Rather than using the ventilation file and the insights of colleagues to acknowledge our jumbled, unpleasant feelings, we focus on all the other demands on our time. It is easy to blame them for keeping us from writing. This is mostly unconscious, but that's how myths work. We will explore how to deal more effectively with stalled projects in chapter 22. For now, notice how feeling "too busy" can be both true and an internally created obstacle.

You can begin to dissolve your beliefs about needing to clear the decks by acknowledging the reality of your life. It is—and probably always will be—demanding. Over just one year, among the five members of my faculty writing group, one of us was in a near-fatal car accident (which required months of recovery); a daughter became seriously ill; a department chair died; elderly parents had multiple crises; an unwarranted lawsuit was filed; heirloom furniture was smashed by a moving company; major dental work was required. Meanwhile, each of us had departmental crises to address and the full complement of conferences, public lectures, and family trips.

Plus we dealt with the usual professional obligations—class preparation, committee meetings, reports, letters of recommendation, and grades. This is just what happens in our professional lives. Yet in spite of all these challenges—major and minor, unexpected and expected—each of the group members found ways to keep in touch with their projects and make progress on them.

Letting go of the delusion that things are going to settle down (soon or someday) frees us to figure out how to secure writing time right now, in the midst of our many current commitments. If your heart sinks at this prospect, it may be because you believe you can't possibly put one more obligation—like writing—into your life right now. It already feels like your life is full to bursting, and you can't imagine adding anything more.

The key to challenging the cleared-deck myth is to remember that our scholarly work is not just one more unwelcome obligation. It is a *voluntary commitment*—what we need to do to be happy and successful in our chosen field. Scholarly writing should be an activity we respect and believe in. It is not just "one more thing." It is the main thing in our professional lives. It can be a pleasant, rewarding thing—once we learn how to give ourselves frequent low-stress, high-reward encounters in a supportive environment with a project we care about.

Our writing times can become a refuge, because every day we can devote ourselves to something we believe in. In securing time for our scholarly work, we enact our commitment to questions and problems that matter to us. This is the life we have worked so hard to be part of. Prioritizing and protecting small units of time each day for our scholarly work is how we honor our commitment to it.

In the chapter on taming techniques, I suggested that we think of our writing projects as pets waiting patiently for their daily walk. If I waited until my decks were clear to walk my dog, she would never get out of the house. It is easy for me to forget that I *get* to walk my dog—it's a privilege, not just another obligation. Sometimes I just have enough time to go around the block with her, but for at least a few minutes each day I can spend relaxed and happy time outdoors with my dog. It decreases my anxiety, it is the right thing to do, and it provides a welcome respite.

This is exactly how writing can feel, if we make it into a valued priority, not just one more obligation. It is a privilege to be able to do our scholarly work in the midst of the many other demands of our profession. When life feels overwhelming, we can give ourselves the solace and refuge of regular writing time. If we connect with our project every day—even briefly—it becomes much easier to accomplish the many other things "on deck" that need to be done.

. . . .

Fear of being criticized can hamper academic writing from conception to submission. At every step of the writing process it leads us to defend ourselves against possible attack. Like the other myths that block academic writing, the "hostile reader fear" can haunt us whenever we sit down to write.

This fear is not unwarranted. Our academic work will indeed be scrutinized by a series of readers. Some of these readers may be highly critical—even snide and vicious. And that will hurt. Taking into account what others might say about our work is a valuable way to make what we write more thorough and comprehensive. But the hostile reader fear goes further—it is a deep, often unrecognized fear of being wounded, maybe even destroyed, by what someone else has to say about our work.

The hostile reader fear can be a major contributor to writer's block. It can silence us completely unless we can find skillful ways to respond to it. As one of my colleagues pointed out, "The easiest way to avoid being told you are a crappy writer is not to write anything at all."

Fear of being attacked also leads us to try (and of course fail) to write something impervious to all criticism. This encourages the worst kind of academic writing—oblique and baroque, pugnacious and grandiose, or mechanical and sterile. No matter what our field, fending off an imaginary hostile reader deflects, inhibits, and impairs our scholarly work.

The academic system is designed to offer continuous scrutiny. If the system is working, our writing will improve through the critical response of others. But the review process is not designed to be warm and fuzzy. It feels—and sometimes is—unsafe. So we need to find ways to work with a review system that can seem cruel and arbitrary, even if its admirable goal is to ensure quality scholarship.

When we're in the grip of the hostile reader fear, submitting our work makes us feel as if we are throwing ourselves to the wolves. Our colleagues can (and may) reduce our best efforts to rubble. Reviewers can (and may) tear our best offerings into bloody shreds. Who can possibly do good work when imagining—and trying to avoid—devastating attacks?

The opposite of the hostile reader fear is the euphoric reader hope. When I was interviewing British literary editor Diana Athill, she told me that much of her job involved telling her writers (including V. S. Naipaul and Jean Rhys) over and over, "Darling, you're wonderful." It was a revelation to me that even the successful writers she edited continually craved affirmation.

Lots of us are like Ralphie in *A Christmas Story*, who dreams his teacher will swoon and write A++++++ on his Red Ryder BB gun essay. Instead she corrects his grammar, gives him a C+, and warns him, "You'll shoot your eye out." We need to find a realistic middle path between our hope for swoons and our fear of humiliation.

In other words, academic writing can trigger two demons we need to find ways to befriend: unrealistic hopes of being understood and admired, and unrealistic fears of being mercilessly attacked. Here are four strategies that can help.

First, we can remember that when our work is evaluated negatively, we ourselves are not being criticized. We need to *depersonalize* the experience, because critical comments are about our scholarly work, not us. Hard as it is to maintain this distinction, it is crucial to our academic well-being. Scholarly work is our chosen craft. It is what we do, not who we are. Someone else's red ink on our drafts is not a direct attack on us. It is just their current response to what we have currently produced. We have not been evaluated; an example of our scholarly work has.

Second, we can *reframe* imagined future criticism as a form of support. Careful critique is a gift, and we should hope for valuable guidance from future readers, rather than simply dreading their cruel comments. When colleagues or reviewers give us detailed feedback, they give us (with little or no compensation) their time and attention. They are helping us find ways to make our work better. While you can't predict what kinds of comments your work will receive, you can write in the hope of receiving helpful feedback. So imagine future criticism as a gift that can strengthen your work, rather than as a persecution.

Your ventilation file can be a third coping strategy. The ventilation file is a safe place to find out exactly what your imaginary hostile reader has to say about your work, since you are probably your own worst critic. Once you *acknowledge the critic-in-your-head*, you've got a lot less to fear. So go for broke: use your ventilation file to express whatever you think really vicious readers might say. Beat them to the punch. Then deal courageously with whatever this (hypothetical) hostile reader tells you.

No advisor, colleague, or reviewer can truly demolish you unless they trigger your own deepest fears about your work. The hostile reader you really need to "invite in for tea" is your own projection. Let the ventilation file express the worst you can imagine, then respond as compassionately as you can. Prove to yourself that you can survive whatever nastiness your imagination can come up with.

A fourth strategy is to *substitute a real person*—supportive and trustworthy—in place of an imaginary hostile reader. This tactic helped me when I was a graduate student. A young professor at another institution knew I was having writing troubles, and he suggested that I write my dissertation "to him." This helped me because he actually valued my topic. My deepest fear was that my dissertation committee would be contemptuous of my attempt to do scholarly work on country music. Deep down I feared they would trash someone studying what they thought was trash. Imagining my professor-friend as a future supportive reader helped me focus on doing the work rather than on my fears of being dismissed or ridiculed. It helped me imagine constructive editing rather than destructive criticism. And it allowed me (mostly) to let go of whatever I was afraid awaited me when I finally submitted my dissertation for the committee's review.

If the hostile reader fear is hampering your writing, try these four strategies. When you find yourself assuming hostility from future readers, realize what you are doing, write about it in your ventilation file, and get back to work.

Why not imagine a helpful (if not euphoric) reader instead? The reality is that no matter what you write, you probably won't be given an A++++, but you probably won't be permanently destroyed either. Respond to your fears of future criticism with these support strategies, and remember that you can survive—even benefit from—what actual readers will eventually offer.

14 } COMPARED WITH X

. . . .

Comparative evaluation is the lingua franca of academe. We have been getting grades since kindergarten, and most of us have done pretty well in this system. We have come to expect that our hard work will always place us at the top of the class.

Then we get to graduate school and find ourselves surrounded by lots of other high achievers, also used to being "the best." We are faced, maybe for the first time, with not setting the curve. This feels like we are not measuring up. Which can lead to the sense that "compared with X" (some exceptionally productive colleague) we are less than and falling behind.

Most writing myths come from beliefs that have some basis in reality. The painful truth here is that you may never again be able to count on "setting the curve" or being "the best." Chances are good that no matter how hard you work, you will be behind someone else, somewhere, on some measure. You may be prolific, but not in the right journals. You may be in the right journals, but not often enough. You may have written a book, but others have written several. You too may have written several books, but they were not published with equally prestigious presses. You may have published ten books with prestigious presses, but they are not having as much influence as someone else's. And on it goes. "Compared with X" always has the power to makes us feel bad.

So the first step in dealing with destructive comparison is to accept that there will always be "better than you" scholars. Your days of setting the curve may be over. You have colleagues who are more eloquent, insightful, and productive than you are. The only solution to this situation is to accept it and let it go. Holding on to comparisons—whether positive or negative—keeps us trapped. Berating ourselves for our perceived writing inadequacies guarantees misery.

But so does taking too much pride in our comparative productivity—the flipside of feeling "less than" is to seek ways to feel "more than." Some of us try to become more productive, more influential, more successful at publication than specific other colleagues. Writing becomes a way to keep score and gloat. It's a way to hold on to that familiar but increasingly elusive top-student status by trying to turn everyone else into also-rans.

Living by comparisons misshapes our character as well as our writing. It puts the focus on outside evaluation (real or imagined) rather than on doing our own best work. Yes, we are always being evaluated, but we need not turn "being the best" into a moral imperative. We stay both "right-sized" and "write-sized" by focusing on making valuable contributions to the field, rather than on how many publications we can crank out compared with others.

There is no single measure of academic writing worthiness. Hiring, tenure, and promotion committees establish guidelines for scholarly productivity that we must of course take seriously, and during professional reviews we get comparative feedback that we must take into account. But don't internalize this feedback either as an accurate assessment of the quality of your scholarly writing or as a measure of your true worth as a human being.

Institutional reviews represent how particular colleagues think you are measuring up against their (often self-interested) interpretation of strategically vague criteria. It is information you need to have to make wise decisions about your perceived success at this moment in this academic circumstance. It is a stressful process, but it need not be debilitating. Accept it for what it is—feedback on where you stand in relation to these people and these institutional norms. Do not let the review process trigger the more personal "compared with X" myth.

This myth is so devastating because it cuts to the heart of who we think we should be as scholars. We want to excel, stand out, and be recognized as particularly worthy. Instead of focusing on our scholarly work as a craft, we come to see it as a measure of our essential worth. That's when our scholarship becomes tangled up in measuring ourselves against selected others in our department, field, university, nation, the world, and the past. We compare their magnificent finished products to our own paltry efforts and feel inadequate.

This obsession with comparison is counterproductive at best and paralyzing at worst. It keeps us focused on someone else's writing strengths and weaknesses while preventing us from feeling safe and comfortable with our own. People differ not only in innate ability, skills, and training but also in what can be called writing temperaments. Some people love to write and do so easily and well. Others dislike writing but have learned techniques that help make it more satisfying. Others resent being "forced" to write, but they find ways to do it anyway. Comparing our own process with that of others who have different writing temperaments is unhelpful. Instead, we can learn to work effectively with who we are, drawing on techniques that enviable others may have mastered.

A premise of this book is that academic writing requires a supportive environment—both externally and internally. Whatever does not produce a supportive writing environment should be identified and protected against. In my role as individual writing coach, I help colleagues identify and experiment with various techniques and strategies. The goal is to help each of them find ways to become their own writing coach.

Would an effective coach berate you for being "worse" or "behind" or "too slow" compared with someone else? Would he or she constantly throw that person's achievements in your face, so that you feel like a hopeless failure? Of course not, because bullying is not motivating.

Would an effective coach make derogatory remarks about your talented peers, so you can find a way to feel better about your own abilities? Would he or she encourage you to cut them down to size so you can feel big? Of course not, because this strategy wouldn't help you develop your own writing skills.

A good coach works with your strengths and helps you figure out how to meet your own goals. The antidote to chronic comparison is to focus on giving yourself what you need in order to do your best scholarly work.

Almost everyone struggles with writing doubts and fears and obstacles, even those who seem to be effortlessly producing great work. I have talked with colleagues who are blocked and colleagues who are prolific, and they describe the same insecurities and anxieties. The difference is that the prolific ones use techniques that work for them. We have similar writing hopes, fears, and struggles, but some of us have found our own combination of effective writing techniques—by focusing on doing our own best work, not on how we measure up compared with others.

Kevin, a participant in a writing workshop at another university, offered me this example of how a simple change in punctuation can release us from the comparison trap. We are always wondering, he said, if we are good enough. But what if instead we know that our work is good and believe that is enough? He illustrated this by writing "Good enough?" and then crossing out the question mark and adding two periods. "Good. Enough." It made all the difference.

To counteract the debilitating effects of comparison, commit to doing your own work with as much skill and integrity as you can. Be pleased, even grateful, that you share a department, university, field, or world with dazzling scholars-who-are-not-you. Learn what you can from them, let them inspire you, but stay connected to your own writing. Remember, no one but you can do your project. Forget about "colleague X," and focus instead on what you can do for your project. Make it good. That is enough.

15 } THE PERFECT FIRST SENTENCE

. . . .

Some of my colleagues can't begin writing until they have found the Perfect First Sentence. They spend hours seeking just the right words, tinkering with a single sentence that never quite captures what they are trying to say. Frustrated and discouraged, with little to show for their hours of intense effort, they eventually conclude that they "just can't write."

If this is you, there are several techniques that can honor your desire to get the words just right but give you more effective routes to achieving that goal. The key to dispelling the "perfect first sentence" myth is to understand that there are at least four phases to writing: prewriting, drafting, revision, and editing.

The good news is, if you struggle with the Perfect First Sentence myth, you will enjoy the last two phases: revising and editing. But what you need first are effective ways to prewrite and draft. Obviously you can't revise and edit material that doesn't yet exist. Prewriting and drafting let you create rough approximations of material that you *then* polish into a finished product.

All writing requires prewriting. This is the phase after your content elements have been gathered but before you know exactly how you are going to arrange and present these elements to readers. It is a crucial, invisible, and often underappreciated element in all forms of writing.

Figuring out what we should say—our written content—requires rumination. We need to ponder and explore possibilities, because all writing projects can be organized in many different ways. Perfect First Sentence types are trying to do this in their heads instead of on the page. The search for the right sentence is actually a ruminative process—trying to get the ideas and claims and evidence into effective sequential order. What makes it into a myth is your misguided belief that once you find the right place to start, the whole piece will magically fall into place.

Staying in your head, waiting for a first sentence to coalesce into a finished structure, doesn't always work. Prewriting offers a different approach. It lets you consider various options for content and structure by filling the page or screen with a number of (temporary) possibilities. These ideas and phrases will be—and should be—imperfect, incomplete, and inadequate. These fragments are a crucial first stage in the evolution of your project.

My high school teachers considered a formal outline to be the only effective prewriting strategy. It was (and still is) excruciating for me to do a linear Roman-numeral plan—it is far too rigid and structured. Instead I use a pen on paper to scrawl disordered ideas or phrases, with lots of arrows, circles, and cross-outs. This gets me in touch with some of the elements of what I think I want to say. It's akin to the "word-cloud" system recommended for corporate brainstorming. My prewriting process gets thoughts out of my head and onto paper in a sloppy nonlinear form. It's a template to get me rolling, even if I barely refer to it later on.

If formal outlines work for you, then by all means keep using them. But if they feel awkward or forced, explore other options. If my handwritten scrawl system seems too old-fashioned, use the screen—a silly font or vibrant color may help you throw down some prewriting elements. Or try putting key words or phrases on Post-it notes or 3×5 cards—these can be rearranged until they seem good enough for now.

Another suggestion is to start with free writing that "doesn't count." Peter Elbow offers a description and specific example in his essay "Freewriting and the Problem of Wheat and Tares."[1] Write whatever comes to your mind about your topic without worrying about syntax, eloquence, grammar, spelling, or punctuation. Do not reread—just go full out. Do not reflect or edit, just talk it out on paper without worrying about coherence. Get the words out there. Focus not on "exactly where I need to start" but on what you have to say in this section. Let the whole mess stand as a temporary first sentence because you know you will be back, later, to create an actual first sentence, once you have completed your first rough draft.

What you want to write, of course, is not the first sentence but a first

1. Chap. 3 in *Writing and Publishing for Academic Authors*, ed. Joseph M. Moxley and Todd Taylor (Lanham, MD: Rowman and Littlefield, 1997).

draft. And it can and should be a real mess. Anne Lamott, in her classic literary writing advice book *Bird by Bird*, talks about "shitty first drafts." I encourage you to adopt her attitude. Know that writing involves stages and that the prewriting and drafting are supposed to be embarrassing messes. No matter how disgusting your first draft is, it still gives you what you need: something solid to develop and polish.

If you struggle with this myth, you need to corral your perfectionism long enough to get your words out, then turn it loose in the revising and editing phases. The scrawled template, sentence fragments and crummy first draft are verbal clay that you fling onto the page in big chunks. No one else will ever see them, and you will shape them into something acceptable later on. But for now you are throwing stuff down, quickly and sloppily, just to pile up some content.

Instead of struggling to find a single sentence that will lead to a perfect final piece, accept that all writing starts out messy. It becomes orderly through revising and editing. Which means that the antidote for the Perfect First Sentence myth is to let yourself fully participate in these two phases of intentional imperfection—prewriting and drafting.

Sloppy writing can provoke overwhelming anxiety in some people. If you are a perfectionist, you hate to write badly, and it feels humiliating, even in the early stages. You want to make sure that your words are "right" at every step of the process, which is why you spend so much time in front of an almost empty screen, polishing and rearranging a few sentences over and over. This is why you get more and more frustrated about how long it takes for you to pile up pages.

Happily, you have just the skills you need to be a gifted reviser and editor. Your perfectionist tendencies can be fully deployed after you have forced yourself to throw down some slop in the general direction of your topic. During revising and editing you will finally be free to honor your deflected desire to get your words exactly right. In revision you can go back to your pile of sentences and choose a good place to start. You might find a nearly perfect first sentence anywhere in your draft—often my first sentence shows up toward the end of my draft, when I've shown myself what I want to say.

During revision, writers tighten and rework—cutting out swaths of words that don't fit, finding an unexpected theme and developing it, or just eliminating or swapping paragraphs to make things flow better. My revised draft doesn't have much in common with my scrawled notes—but so what? I've managed to create solid material to work with, because I was willing to throw down imperfect approximations of what I was hoping to say.

When editing, you get to polish and perfect your almost-ready-to-be-seen-by-others draft. This can be done section by section, or it can wait until you have a complete version. The point is to keep your perfectionist polishing completely separate from the prewriting, drafting, and revision processes. Get yourself through the anxiety-inducing acceptance of imperfection in the earlier phases, so that during editing you can give free rein to all your perfectionist desires.

The reward for prewriting and drafting is that you (finally!) get to tinker and polish. Now is your chance to make each sentence as clear and concise as possible, with solid grammar, spelling, and punctuation. You can erase all signs of your incoherent prewriting and crummy first drafting and the tentative changes of your rewriting phases. Remember, all good writing starts in messiness so it can head toward perfection.

Be grateful that you are the kind of person who likes to make words come out right. This is a trait that all good writers have and that all academic writing needs. But to be both good *and* productive writers, we must find ways to bracket our desire for perfection until the final phases of the writing process. The place to start is not with a perfect sentence but with some approximations that, through revision and editing, become exactly what we were trying to say all along.

16 } ONE MORE SOURCE

s a young woman, social reformer Jane Addams spent several years trying to find ways to be of service to society. But her preparatory period, she later came to believe, went on far too long. She was too caught up in plans, unable to move forward into action. In her memoir *Twenty Years at Hull House*[1] she borrows a phrase from Leo Tolstoy and calls this "the snare of preparation."

Spending too much time preparing, rather than getting started, happens often in academe. We can spend months, even years, "getting ready" to write. In scholarly writing there is no natural boundary to the amount of literature we can review, and it can feel safer (and more interesting) to be getting ready to write rather than plunging into actual writing.

Before starting this section I was tempted to reread books by and about Addams and track down the original quote from Tolstoy. I thought about gathering secondary sources on both Tolstoy and Addams to make sure that I understood exactly what each meant. I also considered doing an Internet search to make sure that no one else is using "the snare of preparation" in some other way that would make me look uninformed if I didn't note it here. I could even have gone in search of another, better phrase to use in this section in case "the snare of preparation" was too obvious, or outdated, or obscure, or clichéd.

In other words, I could have succumbed to the myth of One More Source. We get stuck in the "snare of preparation" when we delay writing until we have gathered even more of what might be relevant scholarship. We stay in "gather and organize" mode, delaying writing and thereby missing deadlines and feeling both incompletely prepared and behind. The snare of preparation keeps us trapped in getting-ready-to-write.

1. (New York: Macmillan, 1912).

Obviously, we all need to be well grounded in the literature of our field to do our best work. But we can never be fully grounded in it. We live in an information-rich environment with unprecedented access to ideas and evidence. There will always be more scholars to discover, more articles to read, more studies to cite. Beyond this, in our increasingly interdisciplinary era, there will always be different keywords to try, unfamiliar methods to consider, and new knowledge areas to master.

But the "snare of preparation" has been around a lot longer than Google Scholar and interdisciplinarity. One reason we get trapped in reviewing the literature, rather than writing, is that we want to be sure we are truly expert in our corner of our field. We want to really know what we're doing. We don't want to be—or be perceived as—bad scholars. This is a version of the impostor syndrome, a version that we need to acknowledge and befriend rather than try to suppress. Our fear of being unmasked as inadequate underlies our felt need to include every possible source.

It feels easier and safer to be "researching" rather than doing the hard and sometimes scary work of writing. Background research keeps us from feeling anxious, but when it goes on too long it is a form of stalling. So how can we know when we are ready to turn from hunting and gathering to actually making our own contribution to the field? What are the differences between being well-grounded in the literature and being stuck in the snare of preparation?

My experience has been that every literature review eventually becomes repetitive, even predictable. I know it's time for me to switch from gathering to writing when the sources fall into familiar patterns.

I start out feeling overwhelmed by all the books and articles and ideas and authors I've never read or even heard of. But because I enjoy the quest itself—the seeking and finding of books and articles, the process of discovering how an area of inquiry develops and coalesces and comes apart—I happily download articles, browse shelves, and order books from the library. At first their bibliographies offer me lots more sources to find, but toward the end of the process they offer me recurring familiar landmarks.

The hunting and gathering helps me recognize Big Names and Major Concepts, Intractable Schisms and Ongoing Debates. But eventually the thrill of the hunt settles into a less exhilarating more-of-the-same. Then it is time to reread, closely and carefully, and choose which sources I really want to draw on and therefore cite.

When this happens, you are ready to create a draft of a literature review. This is preliminary, a way to organize content in order to run it by trusted mentors who really know your field. If you are stuck in search-and-collate mode, stop searching. Become willing instead to put together a description of what you have already gathered. Show it to a few colleagues to see if you are on the right track. Are there obvious absences? Who haven't you read? What else needs to be included? Are you conversant enough with the main aspects of this particular corner of the field?

This draft literature review allows you to organize and bracket the gathering phase. It leaves room for more sources that may come to your attention. Colleagues will have suggestions before you submit, and a good review process should give you even more options to evaluate and incorporate before final publication.

Good scholarship is open ended—an ongoing conversation. Your goal is to become part of the conversation in your corner of the field. So rather than fearing that you are missing something as you try to review "all" of the literature, gather enough to let others help you find additional pertinent information, and move ahead with your project.

Knowing we can and will find more is key to letting go of the One More Source myth. To be productive in academic life, we need to accept that we can never become completely conversant with all relevant literature before we publish. It is just not possible. Instead, we need to become conversant enough to interact productively with others in our area through presenting, writing, and publishing.

Our job isn't to become impervious to critique but to participate effectively in the scholarly conversation. This requires actually understanding and mastering carefully selected sources rather than piling up an impressive list of references. There is one certain way to look like a bad scholar in your literature review—not by missing a source but by misunderstanding a source. Be selective, and understand all the relevant sources you choose to cite.

Early on in my academic career I wrote an essay with a misleading title. It explored why social critics wrongly (I believed) presumed that fans were needy and unstable and pathetic. I titled it "The Pathology of Fandom: The Consequences of Characterization." I was arguing that fandom is normal, not pathological. But a distressing number of speed-readers cite the essay to support the very argument I critique. This means they look like bad scholars to me, and to anyone who has read and understood my work. Wanting to include all possible fan studies citations, they just threw mine in, without (apparently) even glancing over it, to be sure they had everything covered.

So watch out for the temptation to cite every possible source. Be sure you truly understand the articles and evidence you are choosing to use, and gather enough to do a first draft of your review. This gives you something to show others and increases the likelihood that you will see familiar patterns—which means you really are ready to start writing.

If you have been "getting ready to write" for months or years and doing a preliminary literature review feels impossible, maybe your fear of missing an important source is really about something else. Perhaps it is a cover for other myth-fueled fears—like being excoriated by hostile readers, exposed as an impostor, or failing to write a magnum opus. If this is the case, then no amount of citation gathering will help you start writing. Put the literature review aside and address your actual fears.

The idea that there is one more source out there—crucial to the ultimate success of your project—can delude you into thinking that you are being productive when actually you are just ensnared in preparation. Give up the dream of complete expertise and replace it with a commitment to becoming conversant with what you need to know to write this particular piece right now. Incorporate the truly relevant sources into a draft literature review, and get on with your writing.

Part Four

. . . .

MAINTAINING MOMENTUM

It would be wonderful if by using the three taming techniques, securing our time, space, and energy, and working skillfully with our most troubling writing myths, we could write easily forevermore. Alas, this is one more myth—that writing momentum, once achieved, never leaves us.

The truth is that we can chug along cheerfully for weeks and then suddenly (or gradually) begin to falter. We realize that we haven't written for days, or that what we're working on isn't going anywhere. We feel disconnected from our project or lost in a thicket of options. We get feedback that disheartens us; we get revision requests that stop us cold. If we don't address these circumstances skillfully, we find ourselves not just in a lull but stalled, perhaps permanently. We forget our writing tools and succumb yet again to our writing myths. We start telling ourselves stories that stand in the way of writing progress.

In this section we explore ways to maintain writing momentum by working effectively with our naturally fluctuating focus, motivation, and commitment. We accept that sometimes writing ebbs, then flows, feels easy and then hard, grinds to a halt and then suddenly gushes out. There are ways to work with these variations to make sure that we don't get stuck and discouraged.

Not all ebbs are stalls. If you find yourself losing momentum, the first thing to do is go back to basics. Are you still using the three taming techniques? Are you still securing your time, space, and energy? What is showing up in your ventilation file? Which writing myths are you "taking for granite" once again?

If the basics are still in place but you are not making comfortable progress, you need to explore and apply specific concrete steps to restore your writing momentum. This section offers suggestions that can keep your writing moving forward, no matter what.

. . . .

In my department's capstone course, we give our undergraduate majors the chance to do an individual project of their own
choosing. Our only requirement is that it make a contribution
of some sort to the world. We urge each student to draw on their
personal interests and come up with a project that really matters to
them. But over and over most of them suggest boring, generic projects
that they don't really care about.

Why? Given this chance to research and write about something
that is personally meaningful, why do they choose something that
doesn't truly excite them? And in our own academic careers, why do
we do the same? All the writing techniques in the world can't help us
if we choose to work on academic writing projects that we don't really
want to do.

We are more like these undergraduates than we realize. Many students chose, long ago, to keep their schoolwork separate from their
"real" lives. They don't trust that mixing the two is allowed. They have
succeeded so far by choosing safe, dull, easily doable projects. Whatever their personal passions may be, they keep them safely bracketed
from "school."

Consciously or unconsciously, we may be using this same strategy.
We may believe that our scholarly work is not supposed to be personally meaningful. Our mentors may have told us to wait until we're professionally established before pursuing the research questions that
truly interest us. So when is that, exactly? Before we get tenure? After?
When we are promoted to full professor? Get an endowed chair? Or
retire?

Under the pressures of a tight job market, many of us strategically
choose our initial research areas to ensure professional success. Then
we stay too long with the same safe choice so that we have a consistent research trajectory (or "academic brand") for the job search or
tenure process. Even after tenure, when we presumably have the free-
dom to go in any direction we want, we may stick with the generic and

familiar. We can continue, like my students, to overlook or bracket our passions.

This is a mistake if our goal is to become happy and productive academic writers. Remember the last part of that summary advice sentence: brief, frequent, low-stress/high-reward encounters with *a project we enjoy*. It is hard to enjoy a scholarly project that we don't really value or don't believe makes a contribution, or that doesn't connect with our genuine interests.

It can be tempting to choose methods and projects that do little more than add lines to our vitae. But in my experience, the careerists who choose projects they don't care about will become contemptuous of themselves and their field. Eventually they can't push themselves any longer. They can't bear to do another project they don't really care about. Sadly, they have had little or no experience choosing projects they *do* care about.

Through trial and error I developed a technique that helps my undergraduates devise projects that truly engage them. I'm now using this technique with faculty colleagues. It is how I help them figure out why they are stalled or help them decide which project they want to work on next. Most of the evidence I can offer here is anecdotal, but "following the lilt" helps locate which project, or parts of a project, a writer really wants to do.

"The lilt" is a quality of voice. Almost everyone's voice gets more energetic or musical when they are describing something that engages them. Almost everyone's voice gets flat and mechanical when describing something they "should" like but really don't. You can train yourself to hear "the lilt" (or its absence) when someone else is talking about their project.

Using the lilt technique, you pay attention not just to what someone is saying but to how they are saying it. You will hear wisps of enthusiasm, as well as moments of rote recitation, in the tone and quality of their voice. Listen for, note, and then follow up on the moments of lilt. These moments identify which projects, or parts of projects, truly excite them. And which ones don't.

This technique involves give-and-take. The listener says something like "I think I hear a lilt when you talk about X." The speaker then talks more about X, while the listener asks more questions, noting not only the words but also their tone. Most listeners can hear when the speaker's voice sounds matter-of-fact and when it sounds musical.

By continuing to listen deeply and ask follow-up questions, listeners can guide speakers to the parts of their proposed or current project that sound "lilty"—like they truly care. The speaker hears but also feels the difference. Enjoyable projects feel energetic and buoyant; obligatory projects feel enervating and leaden. In the give-and-take of "following the lilt" the listener can identify and explore what matters most to someone in a stuck or avoided project.

I think all of us in academic life could use this kind of collaborative guidance. We can learn how to help each other "follow the lilt" as we decide what to work on next, or how to reframe a project that has gone stale, or how much we are willing to revise in order to resubmit something we've already written.

But most of us still go it alone, trying as best we can to figure out what we "should" do all by ourselves. We don't always get wise counsel from our mentors; we don't always receive sensitive feedback from our colleagues. We may even believe we don't (or at least don't yet) have the right to do projects that interest us. Many of us dutifully choose sensible, uninteresting projects because, like my undergraduates, we can't allow ourselves to take on only the projects that truly engage us.

I recently advised a brilliant young colleague, newly tenured, who had just been offered a chance to coedit a book based on a seminar she had organized, as well as coedit a potentially influential new book series. Each opportunity involved working with prestigious scholars in her field. She already had a contract for her second book (articulating her own new approach to her field) and she had been offered a chance to contribute to an innovative new online venture with a major academic press. Which of these many opportunities should she commit to? Based on her complete lack of lilt, I advised her to withdraw from both coediting projects. The quality of her voice made it clear she should focus on what she is most eager to be doing in the coming months—her second book and the online project. Yes, coediting could enhance her visibility and contribute to her field, but it would also deflect her from what she truly wants to be doing.

Like so many aspects of our profession, choosing among possible scholarly projects is needlessly mystified. We often stumble into writing commitments rather than carefully choosing them. Especially early in our careers, we are flattered to be asked, or feel obligated to a senior scholar, or are tempted by what we are told will be a reputation-enhancing opportunity.

Getting bogged down by undesirable projects often happens with collaborative work, where what looks like an easy publication becomes a difficult, obligatory, and draining slog. Like many others, I have become entangled in collaborative projects that have hindered the pursuit of my own work for precious years. The fact that someone asks us to edit or coauthor (even with promises that it will be quick, easy, or career enhancing) is never a reason to commit to a scholarly project. Why agree to do projects that are only vaguely interesting to us, or that yoke us to the work of others at the expense of our own, or that use the same data and methods to support familiar arguments? Far too many of us find ourselves, often with the best of intentions, agreeing to what we don't really want to do. Of course we eventually lose momentum. Who wouldn't?

The belief that we should agree to all publication opportunities, no matter how trivial or uninteresting or tangential, eventually backfires. The sow's ear does not become a silk purse, and we know it. We obligate ourselves to see it through and squander precious writing time and energy trying to work on an uninteresting topic, often with distracted or unmotivated colleagues, while our own scholarly work gets delayed or pushed aside.

We all deserve better, no matter what stage of academic life we are in. As graduate students, we should be addressing the questions that drew us to our field, the ones that keep us reading and thinking. As junior faculty, we should be excited about the scholarly community we are joining, eager to work with students and colleagues who share our interests and approach. As senior faculty we should feel proud of what we've accomplished and eager to keep making our own contributions—in ways that excite us—to our students, our field, and our profession.

If we don't feel these ways, then it's possible that we've trained ourselves to bracket our own intellectual passions in order to do whatever is required to get us through. We are surviving, not thriving. We are enduring, not flourishing. Which means that we are missing the chance to do work that really matters to us. The kind of work we will be proud of years from now, when we look back on how we've spent our academic lives.

So when you find yourself bored, stalled, and discouraged in your writing, talk with colleagues who can help you find your lilt. It's fine—maybe even better—if they don't know your research area. This means they will be able to stay focused on the tone, not the content, of what you are saying. Talk to them about what first drew you to the field, or what matters most to you about your research area, or what you hope to accomplish with your current choice of possible projects. Let them listen for the lilt so they can help you identify what matters to you. Then do the same for them.

Most of us learned to write under deadline pressure. Many of us make it through graduate programs and even through tenure by forcing ourselves to sit and write for hours and hours until we are finished. Then we collapse, exhausted.

This is binge writing, which turns writing into a needlessly grueling—and intermittent—effort. It makes us feel like writing-warriors and turns our project into an enemy fortress. To get started, we have to vault over the protective walls or ram through the locked gates. Faced with such an exhausting effort, wouldn't we rather check e-mail, get that memo out, do a little more research, or even finish up some grading?

When we finally do manage to get rolling on our writing, we are afraid to stop. We feel like we need to blaze through as long as we can, as hard as we can, because who knows when we'll have this momentum again? The deadline is looming, the muse is with us, and we can't afford to stop! We know how much effort it took just to get started, so we think we have to keep writing until we have worn ourselves out. We write as much as we can, throwing down words until our time is up. Our writing bouts end only when we can't go on any longer. We abandon the project until we can muster the energy for the next exhausting battle.

We don't have to write this way. It makes us miserable and it doesn't work. We don't have to gird our loins and fight our way into writing. We don't have to keep at it until our time and energy run out. Our writing myths support this martial approach; our experiences as students pulling all-nighters to meet writing deadlines may be keeping it in place. But productive academic writers rarely do binge writing. They know how to create and sustain writing sessions without turning them into siege warfare.

Productive writers find ways to guide themselves into writing. They stop each session before they are completely drained. They leave themselves reentry points to get started next time. They find ways to invite themselves back to their desks, where they have left suggestions for what needs to be done next. They trust that words and insights will show up once they sit down for their regular and rewarding writing time.

One of my most productive colleagues is a morning writer who schedules his classes and administrative work for afternoons and evenings. He describes waking up, making a cup of coffee, and then "wandering over to my desk to see what I have to say." Most mornings, he says, he's not sure he has much to offer, so he mentally prepares himself to be unproductive. But he sits down anyway and reads over what he left for himself the day before—the rough beginning of what might become the next paragraph. And to his daily surprise, he finds he might have a little something to add.

He left off knowing where he wanted to head next. He says he doesn't always follow his own suggestion—sometimes he revises instead or finds another path to follow—but his ending notes have served their purpose. Within a few minutes of heading over to his desk, without expectations, he is once again absorbed and engaged. He has a productive hour or two of writing, all because he invited himself to find out if he had anything to say. He used his own suggestion, left at the end of his previous session, to get himself started.

Rather than having to storm the fortress, he strolls through the garden gate he left unlocked. Instead of attacking his project with grim determination, he spends a few hours weeding, planting, and arranging words. When he is pleasantly tired—but before he is drained—he marks a place to wander in the next day.

Even famous fiction writers need daily routines to lure themselves into writing. Some rare writers (like Ray Bradbury and Barbara Kingsolver) wake up awash in words and can't wait to get to their desks. But many others, like Maya Angelou (who rents a motel room) and Haruki Murakami (who runs ten miles after each morning's work), create routines to keep themselves connected to their project. They honor their need to begin with ease and end with energy.

In a famous interview, Ernest Hemingway tells us how to end our writing sessions.[1] "You write until you come to a place where you still have your juice and know what will happen next and you stop." Academic types aren't full-time writers, and we don't need to keep in touch with characters or keep a plot going, but as Hemingway suggests, we can and should stop writing while we still have our "juice" and know what we might want to write next.

Most famous fiction writers who have described their daily routines combine relatively rigid daily writing schedules with carefully orchestrated relaxation and restoration. Unlike academics, authors who can write full time don't need to have enough "juice" to also teach well, do effective departmental service, advise and edit graduate students, design studies, and run labs, all while trying to be an available, responsive parent, partner, and friend. Except during summers and sabbaticals, few academics can create a schedule that includes four or five hours of writing followed by exercise, errands, taking a nap, and relaxing with friends.

But we should still design our endings and beginnings to make our writing sessions more pleasant and productive. When my children were young, I would start writing before they woke up. I skimmed what I'd written the day before, including the reentry note I left for myself. I wouldn't expect to "really write" that early, but I could jot down notes—either on the project or in my ventilation file—choosing to stop as soon as one of my two boys woke up. Once I heard a stir, I would leave my desk, help them with breakfast, and see them off to school. Things are much easier for me now that my children are grown. But on writing mornings I still get up early, start with a quick review to "check in," and then break for breakfast before getting back to an hour or two of uninterrupted writing.

Because I don't consider my prebreakfast jottings "really" writing, I don't feel resistance. But it is enough of a beginning for me to believe that my writing is already started, so I feel ready to return to my desk for a few hours. When my writing time is up (because either I have appointments or I'm running out of "juice"), I leave myself a note about where to head next time. Then I shower, dress, and go out the door. I

1. Interviewed by George Plimpton, "The Art of Fiction," *Paris Review* 18 (Spring 1958).

force myself to wait to check e-mail until my writing time is done or I am at my campus office.

For me, a truly productive writing session usually happens only on designated writing days. I have trouble fully concentrating on the days that I teach, even if the classes are in the afternoon. Like many of us, I can't always choose my teaching times, but I try to teach after 11 a.m. on either MWF or T TH, since I'm a morning writer. On teaching days I do not expect to do much more than reconnect and maybe do some brief outlining or revising. Sometimes I surprise myself and do some good work. But I've had to accept that even though I connect with my writing for at least fifteen minutes, class days are rarely writing-productive for me. I'm just too distracted by class-related worries, even after all these years of teaching.

I know I need to show up every day to stay in touch with my project. Because I end with my next beginning in mind, I can easily re-immerse myself and therefore make progress. If I get disconnected from my project, my writing demons gang up on me, and my designated writing days turn into great opportunities to sleep in, or run errands, or catch up on grading and make plans with friends. If I'm not sure where I'm going to start, I'm tempted to check out the day's news and maybe look at e-mail just this once. My commitment to at least fifteen minutes, along with a designated writing time and space with a note to tell me how to reenter the project, keeps me moving ahead.

Once you've found the times of day that you can devote to writing (by recognizing your A time and protecting it), make it as easy as possible on yourself to just show up, even if you don't think you have the time or focus to get anything substantial done. Ease into your writing to see what will happen. When you do get absorbed in your project, don't write until you run out of words. Stop when you still have energy, and leave yourself a note to invite yourself back in for your next writing session.

Let go of the idea that writing requires you to fight your way over the fortress wall, slashing around in a writing frenzy so that you can meet your deadline. Instead, establish a regular and pleasant writing routine that begins with ease and ends with energy, inviting you to keep coming back.

. . . .

L osing your bearings in your writing project is extremely un-settling. This can happen early on, when the trajectory of your argument seems to shift. It can happen in the middle, when you've lost track of the path you thought you were on and can't see another route to follow. Often it happens toward the end of a project, when you can't find your way out of what has begun to feel like a maze of aimless words.

Every writing project, no matter how small or structured, involves blazing our own trail through our chosen material. In the humanities we tend to focus on questions and arguments, in the social sciences on arguments and evidence, and in the sciences on research questions and findings. Good scholarly work adds something new to our understanding. Even if others have explored this territory, no one will ever walk the exact trail we are forging.

We get general orientation from our disciplines: the scientific report, the social science article, and the humanistic essay each has its own professional norms that tell us how to introduce, review, present, analyze, and conclude our written work. Professional norms may offer us guidelines for how to organize our words, but they can't tell us what we have to say or how we can best say it.

Which is why every writer needs what is called a "through-line." A through-line orients us (and our readers) through our particular set of questions, arguments, or evidence. You can imagine it as a clothesline onto which we hang our introductory claims, literature review, analysis, and conclusions. We use our through-line to focus and arrange what we have to say, which helps us (as well as our readers) make sense of the material we are covering. A through-line gives us direction, and it keeps us from wandering onto other possible paths in our circumscribed forest.

The through-line offers a map we hope to follow—it organizes our outline. But a map is just an abstract plan, not the route itself. As many writers discover, the path we are following can disappear on us, sometimes more than once.

This is okay. Losing our way in a project is a necessary part of writing it. Handled effectively, getting lost offers us a chance to do even better scholarly work. Handled ineffectively, it derails and stalls us. When you find yourself lost—uncertain of where to head next—you need to find ways to reorient and move forward.

A colleague in the humanities got lost toward the end of writing her first book. It was not based on her dissertation—she had made the brave decision to use a new project as her "tenure book." Her first-choice academic press is eager to see her completed manuscript. There is pressure on her to get it published before her tenure review. She leads one of our writing groups, and she knows and uses the taming techniques. Yet she spent nearly six weeks of her precious summer writing time floundering—by her own definition, lost.

Fortunately she did everything right. She did not panic. She kept daily contact with her project and made weekly reports to her writing group. She chose a strategy—to "write her way through it"—that has worked for her before. Like an explorer lost in the jungle, she chose to stumble through the underbrush until she found the path she wanted to follow. She has learned that if she just keeps writing, the right new path will appear. She can then drop or revise the material she wrote while lost, since she has now figured out what it is she really wants to say.

What also helped her, toward the end of her frustrating weeks of floundering, was talking with colleagues about the content of her book. She described to them what she was trying to say and how she thought it should fit in with her other chapters. That helped her reconnect with the through-line of the book, as well as remind herself of what she had already accomplished. Fortunately, she was still happy with her overall argument—the problem was what she wanted to say about a particular set of examples that supported it.

Colleagues asked her questions that forced her to explain why she chose her examples and how they might fit. Those angles gave her fresh ways to think about them but not a clear way to address them. Then, a few days later, she "suddenly" came up with an angle that felt right. She was back on track, thanks to having admitted she was lost and letting others help her reorient. She kept close to her project, adopted a "keep writing anyway" strategy, reconnected with her through-line, tried out options through talking with colleagues, and was able to find her lost trail.

When we are lost, we need to stay connected to our project but open to exploring alternative ways through it. It is counterproductive to doggedly stick with an outline that isn't working as our "lilt" and motivation wane. It is also counterproductive to put the project aside indefinitely in the vain hope that a new path will magically appear. A brief, structured break (as I recommend in chapter 22 on stalled projects) can serve us, but it needs to be done skillfully. Dogged persistence, or abandoning hope, prevents us from the creative insights that offer us a better path through our material.

Trust that your floundering can be productive as long as you stay in regular contact with your project. If you have lost your way in your project, identify this as a "lost trail" situation and take a few days to explore one or more of these reorientation techniques:

> *Use a mission statement.* A mission statement defines the focus and purpose of your project. My mission statement for this book is "Offering academic colleagues process-oriented strategies to overcome writing obstacles." Not very poetic, but brief, concrete, and specific, and it (mostly) keeps me from wandering off into summaries of the literature, or style and content advice, or general critiques of academic life. So summarize the purpose and scope of your project clearly and concisely on a 3×5 card. Does the writing you are feeling lost in right now directly contribute to your mission? If it does, you aren't really lost—you may be confused or have deeper reasons for feeling uncertain, but you are still on track. If what you are writing doesn't align with your mission for the project, then you need to either adjust the statement (but save it—see below) or change what you are writing to align with your overall purpose.
>
> *Review old outlines.* Most writing projects have multiple iterations, but with digital technology we need to make a conscious effort to protect access to what we are discarding

or setting aside. I strongly encourage you to find ways to save early outlines and ideas. I handwrite these, so it's easy for me to keep them in a folder. But on my computer I also store false starts and discarded sections in italics at the end of my chapter. These files, later on, may let me rediscover unexplored themes or questions. If I've changed direction in a project, these early abandoned efforts show me what I once thought I was up to. Often it is a path I have forgotten about, at least consciously—a ghost trail, as I describe below. The discarded files offer me guideposts that can get me back on my original track or onto a more productive one.

Review the whole project. When lost, it can be helpful to retrace your steps. Where did you start? Where have you gone? And are you really lost or just getting used to new perspectives? Sometimes we think we are lost when we are instead just entering new and uncertain terrain, and reviewing our path thus far gives us the momentum we need to keep going forward into uncharted territory.

Talk with others. Briefly explain your project—and your current confusion—to careful listeners. We can get lost in our own written words. Screens and sections begin to blur; our various revisions and dead ends are hard to keep track of and feel impossible to organize. We find ourselves writing in circles, repeating ourselves. Speaking aloud about our project to someone else, using everyday language, helps us hear our own through-line. Colleagues can give us fresh insights, because our response to their suggestions—even their wrongheaded ones—helps us hear where we really want to go.

Make an imaginary conference presentation. Reducing your project to a series of clear statements, in sequential order, is a good way to confirm or revise your through-line. State your introduction, main claims and findings, conclusions. You can even make slides. What is missing? Do you need more evidence? Different sources? What can you conclude, given what you've written and want to write? This process can help you see where you're uncertain and show you what your next steps could be.

Any of the above strategies should take no more than a few days. If you try them and still feel lost, then there may be deeper writing issues going on. Again, don't panic, and see if exploring the issues below will help.

Use the right metric. One reason some academic writers get lost is that they have been piling up words without knowing what they want to say or why they are saying it. This often happens when word count or pages produced is our chosen productivity measure. We academics can ramble on for pages, sounding profound without saying much of anything. Good editors, and good readers, will call us on this. So feeling lost can be a sign that we aren't writing thoughtfully even though we are meeting our goals for number of words or pages written. Try shifting to a different productivity metric: time spent or points made or progress on through-line can serve as a measure for each session's progress.

Be sure it fits. Another reason for feeling lost is that you are losing interest in this particular section of the project. You are slogging through it because you said you would or think you should. In this case, use a colleague to help you "find the lilt" in your overall project. If the lilt is still there for the overall project but not for a particular section, rethink its role. If the section bores you, it will likely bore the reader. Does it really need to be in your project? If so, write it as briefly and clearly as you can. If not, then drop the section.

Retrieve your lilt. You may feel lost because the lilt—your energy and interest—is disappearing. This means you are disheartened, not lost. This often happens with writing projects. Sometimes it passes after a day or two (write about it in your ventilation file) and sometimes it doesn't. Go back to your mission statement and through-line, and see if you want to refocus or reframe your project in ways that make it more engaging to you. Go back to your old drafts and false starts. Have you unintentionally left some lilt-worthy ideas behind? If so, look for the ghost trail.

Find the ghost trail. Writing projects, especially long ones, involve an ongoing process of discarding, reshaping, and revising. Sometimes these discarded ideas call to us subconsciously. They are ghost trails: roads not taken, paths not yet pursued. You may be feeling lost because there are better paths you unconsciously wish you had taken. Evidence of these may be in what you've discarded or set aside. Take time to figure out what those "ghost trails" might be, and see if they could work for you now. My ghost trails are almost always more original, insightful, and interesting than the dutiful path I have unwittingly mapped out for myself.

Write courageously. Because our scholarly work is constantly being reviewed and evaluated, we often write circuitously, trying to protect ourselves. We have lost our scholarly nerve, hedging and summarizing the work of others so that we won't have to make any substantive arguments of our own. It is easy to get lost while doing defensive writing, because we are creating an incoherent amalgam of other people's claims, wishy-washy assertions, and portentous platitudes. If this is what is happening to you, accept that you are in the grip of the "hostile reader fear" and find ways to directly and courageously say what you have to say.

Work with the quandary. It is also possible to feel lost because you are actually lost: baffled or confused by the material you are working with. As students we learned how to hide our ignorance. We know how to paper over gaps in our understanding and sound sharp and confident even when we feel dull and unsure. So feeling lost may actually be a sign of (at least for the moment) being out of our depth, in over our head, not sure if we have anything to say. You might be able to "write your way through" to new insights, like my humanities colleague did. But you might instead need to do the hard, necessary, and vital intellectual work of really figuring out what you have to say. Step back from your writing, and set a specific amount of time to rethink your premises, read key sources, ask a few colleagues for their insights. This is how serious scholars do their best work; this is why dealing effectively with writing challenges makes us into better scholars.

When you lose track of what you want to say and how you want to say it, you are right to feel lost. Rest assured that this happens with even the most worthwhile writing projects and even the most senior scholars. Choosing to pile up pages in slavish conformity to an unimaginative outline and a looming deadline might feel like the right response, but this strategy guarantees mediocre, uninteresting work.

If you are feeling lost, I hope you choose to use the above techniques to forge a new and better path through your project's terrain. Writing generates insights for us as well as for our readers. We discover new things not just from our research but also through introducing, reviewing, summarizing, and reporting what we have found. Be prepared for moments of confusion, doubt, and floundering. Don't panic and don't give up. Instead, try these orientation techniques. If these don't help you move ahead, then consider what deeper reasons you might have for losing your bearings.

Writing well is thinking well, because it requires recognizing and eliminating weaknesses, contradictions, elisions, gaps, and misunderstandings. So if you really are lost, don't pretend otherwise. Orient yourself by using these techniques to locate and forge your intellectual path.

. . . .

To identify and address the writing issues that keep us stuck, we need the help of others. Supportive colleagues, individually or in groups, can show us that we are not alone in our writing struggles, while giving us valuable suggestions on how we can move forward. They remind us of what we know but don't act on, and they can see patterns in our thinking that we may be blind to.

Many of us recognize our own writing issues only when we see them operating in someone else. Learning how to listen deeply to what is going on with our colleagues (rather than just waiting for our turn to talk) helps us understand what is going on with ourselves. Writing groups can go beyond just reporting on whether or not we met our goals. Describing what really happened as we tried to meet those goals—how it unfolded and how it felt—helps us identify and address what works and what doesn't, with others who are in the same situation.

Truly effective feedback involves seeing behind the smoke and mirrors we generate when we are struggling. It involves knowing what works and doesn't work for writing productivity and being willing to self-disclose in order to help others. Effective feedback is *insightful*—recognizing what is left unsaid; *informed*—offering techniques that work; and *mutual*—based in shared feelings and experiences.

Most of us generate plenty of seemingly good reasons for why, this particular day or week or month, our writing goals weren't met. It is so easy to justify why writing didn't happen as we planned. When someone is describing how grading or service or another departmental crisis has once again prevented them from writing, listen for what is *not* being said. Notice if there is a recurring pattern of rationalization or obstacles that are identified but never actually addressed. See if there are signs of any of the major writing myths. Watch out for blame—of self or others—and for all-or-nothing thinking and self-pity. Offer insights into what might be really going on, along with suggestions for what might help.

Become someone who knows how to both give and receive effective support for the academic writing process. Learn as much as you can about writing productivity options so that you can recommend them to colleagues in distress. Remind them (and thus yourself!) to protect writing time, space, and energy; to have frequent low-stress/high-reward writing encounters; to recognize and let go of "taken-for-granite" myths; to shape the project so that it truly interests them. As you give this kind of informed feedback to others, you are renewing a commitment to your own productivity practices.

At almost every writing-group meeting I hear something that deepens my understanding of what works (and doesn't work) with writing in general and with my own writing in particular. When colleagues share what is really going on with them, rather than just reporting on whether or not they met their goal, I hear all kinds of things that help me. But they need to be speaking honestly, and I need to be truly listening, open to what they might be able to tell me and not just waiting for my turn to talk.

Not long ago, paying attention to my own reaction to a colleague's sharing helped me tremendously. I thought I was on track and had offered my writing group a perfunctory report—yes, I had met last week's goal and was still on schedule, all was well. When it was his turn to speak, my colleague R. chose instead to detail his pleasant new morning writing routine, rather than just agreeing that he too had met his goals and was on track.

I felt a wave of envy as I listened to him--how did he manage to be so easygoing? Suddenly I realized what was really going on with me: I had become increasingly rigid about my writing schedule. I was meeting my weekly writing goals by telling myself, "Get to that desk! You *know* what techniques work! Do it Do it Do it." No wonder I was beginning to feel resistant—subtly starting to respond to my inner tyrant with a sullen "Why should I? Who says? Don't want to!" That command/resist dynamic is familiar. Self-coercion makes my writing feel like a chore, not a choice.

Noticing how I felt about what he had to say saved me from a likely stall and days of scribbling in my ventilation file hoping to figure out what was going on. His willingness to disclose specific details about his own writing process offered me exactly what I needed that week. I had forgotten (as I often do!) that I could just show up at my desk with curiosity rather than tying myself to the chair in front of it. By the following week I was writing with more ease and cheer, thanks to his self-disclosure of what was working for him, and my willingness to explore my own wave of envy in response.

Similarly, I have seen a gentle question—"Are you feeling on track?" "Was grading [or that meeting or that crisis] really so important?" "Are you still protecting your A time?"—make all the difference. It helps us recognize and deal with what we aren't able to see on our own. This is why I prefer face-to-face meetings rather than various digital forms of writing accountability. Yes, meetings take more time, and are more difficult to schedule, and are seemingly "less efficient." But they give us much richer contexts for what we really need to offer each other— insight into what is going on beneath the surface of our efforts to set and meet writing goals.

As we commit to honing our craft, we can also commit to offering and receiving effective writing feedback. Some of us are particularly good at insight—hearing what is behind a colleague's rationalizations, noting troublesome patterns from week to week, and being willing to speak up about them. Others are better at sharing information— reminding each other of techniques to overcome particular obstacles. And some of us will be best at mutuality—describing our own experiences in ways that spark recognition in others. The best colleagues (in or out of writing groups) will offer all three elements, as needed.

But really hearing the feedback we are given, even if it is insightful, informative, and mutual, isn't always easy. We academics can be a thin-skinned and prickly lot. Instead of truly reflecting on what others tell us, we reflexively refute it, often with lightning speed. "That's not it! That's not me! That's not true!" we may retort when someone suggests that we are stalling, or repeating a pattern, or not seeing things accurately. The more anxious and stuck we are in a writing project, the less we may able to truly listen.

Remember that questions and helpful suggestions are not criticism. Try not to react defensively. Beware of feeling jealous or dismissive of others' writing successes, since that means you could miss learning from their suggestions. My envy could have kept me from hearing what R., my "relaxed writing routine" colleague, had to offer me. Fortunately, his words got through.

I find that writing down key phrases—even if it means asking someone to repeat themselves—helps me remember the suggestions I most need to hear. Even when what they have to say seems unhelpful, I write it down. This gives me the chance to assess its actual usefulness. Sometimes it is exactly the insight, information, or mirror I need; sometimes it is not. But I have given myself the chance to learn from it.

Finding ways to give and get effective writing feedback enacts the craftsman attitude. It offers the insights we need to keep writing productively. So find good writing colleagues, either individually or in a group. Then practice giving and receiving insightful, informed mutual feedback about the academic writing process. It's a way to share the skills we all need to overcome our writing obstacles and continue to hone our craft.

. . . .

The chance to make our work a little—or a lot—better is what the academic review process should offer. But the responses of anonymous reviewers can feel (and sometimes be) misguided, even cruel. Just as we dream of writing a perfect work, we dream of finding a perfect reviewer. We hope to have our work read by someone who understands and likes what we have to say and offers us simple suggestions that truly strengthen the piece.

This ideal critic/teacher/reviewer does not always come our way. During your academic writing career, you will need to maintain your writing momentum in the face of debilitating reviewer comments. You may have your best efforts misunderstood, dismissed, or summarily rejected. Given this possibility, you need to find ways to stay calm and courageous in relation to this inescapable element of academic writing.

As a new book writer, I agonized and drifted for months after receiving what I perceived to be a nit-picking twenty-five-page single-spaced critique from the series editor of my manuscript. I was shocked, dispirited, even stung. My written work had never been so closely critiqued (I'm not sure all of my committee members even read my dissertation). So the editor's packed pages of detailed suggestions felt like an ambush. I contemplated pulling the book or just abandoning it. But eventually I found the will to return to his overwhelming-to-me suggestions. Once I'd distanced myself from my despair, I realized that I could easily incorporate most of what he suggested. When I finally met him, he was warm and enthusiastic. He saw his lengthy critique as a gift to me—evidence of his respect for what I was trying to do. And it was a gift. I just couldn't see it that way at the time. Instead, as a new-to-the-process writer, I felt attacked. The lengthy comments felt humiliating, not helpful.

That early experience showed me that even a supportive review experience, for a book already under contract, can feel terrible. It helped me understand, for the first time, that reviewers are volunteers. They offer their thoroughness, care, and insight to help make our work better. They are giving our work their close attention, and no matter what they end up saying, we need to remember that the review process is an increasingly rare remnant of a gift economy. We should treat being reviewed as receiving a gift, even when it feels otherwise.

The review process reactivates the demons we worked so hard to befriend while we were writing. Reviewers' words can haunt us, turning into a disheartening litany that derails us. Reviewer criticisms can seem to validate the very same myths that keep us from writing—especially the magnum opus myth (wanting to write something magnificent) and the impostor syndrome (feeling like a fraud). They confirm our fears of writing for a hostile reader and make us wish we hadn't even tried.

So be prepared, when you receive peer reviews, for a resurgence of myth-related demons. These fears, seemingly being confirmed by the criticism we receive, can make it extremely challenging to do what we need to do: revise, resubmit, and get our work published. We can sink into self-destructive comparisons, wondering why other colleagues apparently sail through the submission process while we have to revise endlessly. We can waste months, even years, incorporating a body of literature that may or may not really be needed for our piece to find publication. We can forget to drain the drama and believe that thanks to whatever this particular reviewer says, we will never land a job, or get tenure, or be promoted or be respected in our field or ever get published again. Our cover is blown, our life is over, and we might as well crawl under a rock and eat worms.

Some academics stall for years in response to rejections or even to relatively benign revision requests. I know of colleagues who have abandoned or shelved work that could have been published if only they had sent it elsewhere, or if they had just revised and resubmitted as requested. But the reviewer comments ignited writing issues they didn't know how to deal with. Because of the review process, the project came to feel toxic, or dispiriting, or wrongheaded.

Rather than working effectively with this normal reaction to the review process, these colleagues set the project aside until "later." There it festers, in limbo. It stays unpublished or undergoes belated, halfhearted (and therefore unsuccessful) revisions. Worse, it stands in the way of fresh new work. It continues to drain the confidence and resilience needed to keep submitting and thereby publishing.

To maintain our academic writing momentum we need to understand that criticism and rejection are necessary parts of the process, although they are almost always hidden from view. As Devoney Looser documents using her own publication record,[1] every CV hides a record of many rejections. Even the most successful academic has what can be considered a "shadow CV," listing numerous failed attempts to publish, as well as to get grants, jobs, or elective offices.

As academic writers, we need to find effective ways to deal with how easily the review/rejection process triggers our writing fears, myths, and delusions. We need to deploy—with even more commitment—all the techniques we use to write successfully. But we need additional strategies to help us revise and resubmit work that we thought was good but that now feels battered and worthless.

We academics are adept at analysis and critique, but most of us would rather dish it out than receive it. Few of us have learned the art of empathetic criticism, whether applied to our students or to our peers. Too often, given the chance to comment, we brandish our insights like weapons. We need to remember that on the receiving end, the sword of our incisive critique can draw blood.

When you are new to the publication process, or deeply invested in a particular article or journal, or are up against a hiring or tenure clock, or lacking effective mentoring, even the most straightforward revision suggestions can feel overwhelming. That piece you have been slaving over, sacrificing for, working to perfect, has been found wanting. What you need to publish as soon as possible now requires even more time and effort, for reasons you may not understand or agree with.

A first step in dealing with this situation is to drain the drama from the reviewing experience. Stay in touch with the imperfect realities of academic publishing. Journal editors are under pressure to find and keep multiple appropriate reviewers, especially reviewers who are easy to work with and will meet deadlines. Book editors are under

1. "Me and My Shadow CV," *Chronicle of Higher Education*, October 18, 2015.

pressure to find academically sound books that will sell well enough to keep the press afloat. They may not be able to locate ideal reviewers for your piece or to work compassionately with you during your revision process. Learn your discipline's norms from journal editors, conference panels, and colleagues. Demystify the academic review process so you can keep it "write-sized."

Remember that the review process relies on busy, procrastinating, and imperfect people—in other words, our peers. Sadly, the anonymity of the process can open the door for some egregious examples of acting out. Anonymous reviewers can write whatever they want, and sometimes they have axes to grind or turf to defend. They may see you as a stand-in for another colleague they want to cut down to size. They may want you to cite them or their journals or their mentors. They may want you to write the piece they themselves wish they had written. They may just want to show off how much they know. So remember, it isn't always about you. It may not even be about your work that is under review. Still, no matter how cruel or wrong or muddled your review/rejection, you can still make good use of what reviewers have to say.

Feeling attacked, we might want to argue with the journal editor or with the anonymous reviewer, letting them know in stinging detail just how wrong their comments are. Do not succumb to this temptation. Even if a reviewer completely misunderstands your argument and is asking you to revise in pointless or even damaging ways, do not say so. Instead, focus on which revisions the editor is actually asking you to make.

Both book and journal editors want to publish high-quality work. Book editors at reputable academic presses are under less time pressure than journal editors are, and so they can form a longer-term relationship with you as an author. Once your book manuscript has received reviews, a good editor can help you decide how you want to move forward with the advice you receive, especially if the suggestions are contradictory. You as an author have more latitude with books than you do with journal articles.

Journal editors are more at the mercy of whichever reviewers have agreed to read your piece. Editors spend an extraordinary amount of time trying to find and cajole appropriate colleagues into reviewing submissions. Sometimes the editor has to settle for someone who may not be quite right for your work. This puts the editor in the difficult position of needing to respect the reviewer, no matter how cursory or off-track the review, while still supporting potentially worthy submissions from people like you.

So journal submission is an imperfect and sometimes unreliable process, but you can and should find ways to use this painful process to improve your work. This is easiest when you get clear feedback—whether a simple (if wounding) no or an enthusiastic (and extremely rare) yes-just-as-it-is. If your submission is rejected outright, note the reasons, briefly thank the editor for his or her efforts, and express the hope that you can submit a different piece to the journal in the future. Do not brood or dwell on this—instead, let experienced colleagues help you figure out what went wrong, how it can be fixed, and what you should do next.

Evaluate the reasons you got an outright rejection. If colleagues think those reasons are suspect, you can choose submission elsewhere. There are always alternative journals. Remember, however, that the original reviewers may end up reading the article they rejected and resent your unwillingness to incorporate their comments. Ask yourself if it is it worth it to you to make changes in response to the concerns of this specific editor and these particular reviewers before you send an unrevised journal article elsewhere. Consider using your rejected piece as a conference paper, panel, workshop, or book chapter. Much rejected-by-peer-review writing can be circulated through other avenues.

If you are fortunate enough to get your piece accepted with revisions, express gratitude to the editor, confirm and complete the suggested revisions, and send the piece back, maybe even before the requested deadline. Acceptance with revisions is a rare and delightful outcome. Make the most of it. Even if the suggested revisions seem trivial or pointless, do them as well as you can. Foster cordial relationships with both editors and reviewers, whatever they say about your work. Academia is a very small world.

The biggest challenge for writers of journal articles comes with the most common response: "revise and resubmit." Now you have the hope of publication dangling in front of you, but only if you comply with often contradictory, infuriating, or seemingly impossible-to-do-in-this-lifetime revision requests. This is where you are most likely to stall, so this is when you need all the calm and collegial guidance you can muster.

Read through the reviewers' comments and the editor's summary just once, then wait a few days. After your mind has cleared, return to the editorial letter summarizing the reviewers' suggestions for you. Find a trusted colleague, ideally one who has edited journals, to help you decode the editor's letter—what revisions do you actually need to do before resubmission? Editors' letters must be carefully analyzed, because they are trying to respect the reviewers' requests while ensuring that they will receive appropriate quality work for their journal.

Is the editor encouraging you to do all or just some of what each reviewer suggests? Are you willing to make all the changes that the editor (not the reviewers) has requested? If so, make them quickly and send them back with a cover letter that details the changes and expresses gratitude for recommending necessary improvements. If you don't want to make most of the changes—and there need to be really good reasons for refusing them, since the editor and reviewers have already spent much valuable time on your work—choose another venue. But let the editor know as soon as possible that you understand and appreciate the suggestions but will be choosing to submit elsewhere.

If you are unsure of exactly which revisions the editor actually recommends, it is appropriate to contact him or her. But do this only to confirm your understanding of the recommendations. Do not plead your case. The point to remember is that you, the editor, and the reviewers all want the piece to be as strong as possible. Incorporate reviewers' every comment only if the editor tells you to do so, or if you or your trusted colleagues see how following the suggestions will directly strengthen your work.

It is always up to your editor which of the many (often off-the-cuff) reviewer suggestions you need to incorporate, especially for journal articles. If you are being asked to revise and resubmit, your editor believes that subsequent review will result in acceptance of your revised and improved piece. That's why you were asked to resubmit. Detail clearly, accurately, and calmly the changes you've chosen to make. When you disagree with a recommendation, give cogent reasons for leaving things as they are. Be sparing with this option.

Ultimately, it is always up to you to ensure that whatever you publish is as good as you can make it. But because the review process is both emotionally fraught and imperfect, you must let yourself be guided by editors and experienced colleagues. Be willing to rethink and rewrite and restructure your work, but do not turn your carefully written work into something it was never intended to be. Never publish something you are not proud of.

Find the middle path between an arrogant refusal to consider changes and a craven willingness to do whatever it takes to get your work out there. When I was just starting out, I didn't understand my options. I made revisions to articles that I should have fought to keep intact. Looking back, I know I should have submitted elsewhere rather than revising in ways that obscured and deflected what I wanted to say.

One of my biggest publishing regrets, on the other hand, is that I once ignored a prominent scholar's detailed suggestions. He was an expert on a historical figure involved in a section of my third book. My editor wanted to meet her publication schedule, and I was ready to get on to new writing projects. I knew that the scholar's suggestions were based on his deeper knowledge, but they were tangential to my overall argument. It would have taken me months to incorporate them. So my editor and I agreed that I didn't need to take most of his suggestions.

Years later, I regret that I refused the gift of this generous colleague's painstaking critique. Making the revisions he suggested would certainly have improved my book. No matter what my editor wanted me to do and how tired of the project I was at the time, I should have had the strength and courage to incorporate his suggestions—his gift to me.

I have also received my fair share of vague, contradictory, or misguided reviews. But even those helped me improve my writing. Misreadings by reviewers tell me where and how I've been unclear. Even snide or denigrating comments (once I depersonalize them) can help me revise my work. They force me to figure out, and possibly clarify, the nature of the disagreement. A nasty review can show me the need to acknowledge a point or perspective I did not realize I had ignored.

Over the years I've come to realize that sometimes reviewers just want the chance to show off—to me, to the editor, to other reviewers. These kinds of reviewers are using the process to showcase their own expertise rather than to find ways to improve your manuscript. Such grandstanding can be useful; self-important experts can still offer insights that help our work. Just don't be fooled into thinking that you have to master a whole new field because the reviewer has showcased his knowledge of it. Focus instead on what your editor thinks you actually need to do.

Give up your secret dream of being fully understood and fully agreed with during the review process. Accept that the process can trigger all your writing issues. Stay open to and respectful of the potential improvements reviewers are suggesting. In the very small world that is your corner of the field, enact your appreciation by letting the review process improve your work.

. . . .

Over the course of every long writing project you will encounter unexpected stasis—a loss of writing momentum. You can't identify any outside causes (although you could surely find some!), and you may not even be sure how long it has been going on. But something has gone amiss. Writing that once was moving along relatively smoothly, mostly on schedule, has ground to a halt.

Stalling can be frightening, especially when you have mapped out a plan to meet ever-nearing deadlines. But stalls happen and are perhaps inevitable. We need to learn to work with these unsettling periods, because even stalling can end up helping our work.

I have encountered at least four types of stalls in myself and in others. Each type requires different antidotes. These four stalls are writing lulls, psychic resistance, structural problems, and profound loathing. You can figure out which one(s) you are dealing with by applying the various antidotes, in serial order.

If you are dealing with a stalled project, go back to the three taming techniques. If brief daily project contact, using a project box and ventilation file, feels okay but not energizing, then you are probably experiencing a simple *writing lull*. Writing energies ebb and flow, especially after you have just met a deadline, or have been asked for revisions, or are ending a stint of productivity. If you are losing motivation, don't keep forcing yourself to write. Instead, consider taking a deliberate and structured writing vacation.

Briefly step away from the project, but first make it ready for your return. Review, condense, make notes; do whatever it takes to say "bon voyage" for now and then "welcome back" after your short break. Make a conscious choice not to write (or brood and worry about deadlines) for a set amount of time. I think a week is ideal; longer than a week is possible but risky. For whatever brief and defined time you choose, let yourself off the writing hook. Commit to putting your project out of your mind.

What this separation allows is a respite. You consciously let go of your writing routine, and, more important, you let go of the self-recrimination that stalling can trigger and deepen. A brief, structured break allows you to replenish your writing energy, giving it a chance to reaccumulate. It can be invigorating for yourself and for your project. If project-related ideas come to you during your "writing vacation," jot them down. Your goal is to come back from your brief break refreshed and renewed.

If when you return you are still feeling stuck, then you are not in a lull but in a second type of stall: *resistance*. Use your ventilation file. Stop trying to make progress on your project until you identify what you are telling yourself about it and about yourself. Review the writing myths—magnum opus; cleared deck; impostor syndrome; fear of hostile reader; compared with X; the perfect first sentence; one more source. Resistance suggests that you need, once again, to drain the drama and develop a more craftsmanlike attitude.

If these efforts still don't work, it is possible that you are not in a lull or in resistance. Taking a break or letting go of myths may ameliorate things but won't get you rolling again. You are stalling because (at some level) you know there is something intrinsically wrong with the project. You need to fix what has gone wrong in order to get moving again. Stalling is a signal that you may be dealing with the third option: a *structural stall*. Something is off, but it's not you, it's the project.

Continuing to batter away at a writing project that feels structurally off will waste your time and drain your energy. Forcing yourself to stick with your schedule or outline or metrics deepens a structural stall and deflects needed insights. What you really need, if you are in this kind of stall, is to reformulate the plan you have been following. Reappraise what you are trying to create, with the help of a trusted colleague. Apply the orienteering techniques detailed in chapter 19, "Finding the Lost Trail." Where is the lilt that shows what really engages you? What does your project need right now? Stay curious and flexible, exploring alternate ways to focus or develop or frame your project. This process is the opposite of "gutting it out."

When I was writing my dissertation, I squandered many months in an unrecognized structural stall. For my prospectus I had created a chapter outline to analyze the commercialization of country music in the 1950s and 60s. My plan was to begin with a chapter on theoretical and methodological issues in media production, followed by a second chapter on the history of the popular music industry. From there I intended to focus on the history of the country music industry in particular, using Patsy Cline's recording career as a case study of how institutional forces shape popular culture, and to end with conclusions about how popular culture commercialization unfolds.

I hadn't taken into account how the process of writing changes what we know, understand, and believe. That's why our projects can and should mutate, taking on shapes and directions we can't foresee. In my case, my dissertation outline was based on premises I no longer believed. It was taking me somewhere I no longer wanted to go—but I didn't consciously realize this.

I stalled when I started writing the second chapter, on the history of the popular music industry. It suddenly seemed beside the point. But the chapter was in the dissertation proposal, still seemed necessary, and incorporated many months of diligent background research. I kept slogging away at it until I stalled and couldn't get rolling again. Then one amazing day I realized that I could—and should—drop the chapter altogether.

My dissertation was no longer a case study in how industrial processes commercialize authentic forms of popular culture. It had become instead an exploration of how industry participants understood authenticity in country music in relation to what they thought was happening in the industry. I didn't need a chapter detailing changes in the popular music industry as a whole. My structural stall had been an indicator that I needed to refocus my dissertation on articulating the role that beliefs, rather than presumed "institutional forces," play in the mediation of culture. That became the new mission of my dissertation, and it made it much more interesting to me and ultimately much more useful to the field of media studies.

Academic writing allows us to include or leave out whatever our project needs to make it stronger. We take the advice of others, of course, but in the end we are the only ones who can sense when something is truly amiss. It wasn't that I was too lazy to write an industry history—I had done the background research and mastered the relevant information, so it was just a matter of organizing and summarizing what I knew. It was that at some level I realized that the chapter didn't fit. It wasn't relevant to what the project had become. The stall helped me discover what I really wanted to say. As soon as I dropped the chapter, I saw how my dissertation embodied a new, more interpretive approach to the study of culture production.

If you are stopped and you have had no success using the strategies for "lull" and "resistance" stalls, it is possible that you have valid structural reasons for losing momentum. If you can figure out what has gone wrong and set it right, you will move forward with new insight, new scholarly contributions, and therefore new energy.

Figure out whether you are just in a writing lull and need a vacation or whether you are experiencing writing resistance and need to deal with the myths that block you. If neither is the case and you are still floundering, you may be experiencing a structural stall. If so, you are in luck. Reframing the project will simultaneously fix the stall and improve your work.

These are my suggestions for how to deal with three of the four kinds of stalling. But what about the most toxic and debilitating writing stall—full out, intractable, relentless *loathing*? That deserves a section all its own.

23 } RELINQUISHING TOXIC PROJECTS

....

What if all your stall-fixing strategies don't get you moving again? What if nothing you try releases you from the grip of unrelenting loathing for your project in any form? If every effort you make to rest from, reconnect with, or reframe your project leaves you feeling more hostile to it, then you are in a toxic stall. I believe your best option is to relinquish the project. Making this choice will free you to find something else to write.

I know that this is terrifying advice—especially if you are ABD or on the tenure clock. But I believe you need to keep "project relinquishing" as a viable writing option. It can even save your academic career.

Most of the unhappy academics I know (and I have known many) are holding on to a toxic stalled project. Their project becomes an ever-more-cumbersome albatross that deflects and even destroys their professional well-being.

I once had a tenured colleague who spent many years describing a book that never appeared, even as articles. He said he was "not ready" for it to be seen in draft form, so during a series of professional reviews, he offered successive (but not substantially different) outlines. This became excruciating for us, his departmental colleagues, because we wanted to believe his increasingly threadbare cover story about a book-in-progress. His humiliation, and our enabling of it, went on for over twenty years. He published little else during that time, and he retired saying he was looking forward to finally having time for "the book." Nothing has come of it.

I have another talented colleague who can no longer even mention the ambitious book project he began (decades ago, as an energetic junior scholar) with the support of a prestigious national fellowship. He has been stalled since then, with only a few related articles reaching print. He left teaching for full-time administration.

Many years ago, my father (a psychology professor) signed a contract to write an introductory textbook he was never able to complete.

His undone book shadowed our childhood and prevented him from moving forward on his many other ideas, because he always felt that he should be "working on the book." The publisher even paid for an avocado-green IBM Selectric typewriter (cutting-edge technology at the time) to help him write it. One editor offered to have my father's class lectures transcribed so he could then turn the transcripts into chapters. But my father was never able to move beyond successive, copious outlines and plans. It was his toxic stalled project that he was never able to complete or relinquish.

Academic culture includes scores of ABDs who talk about, think about, dream about, but never actually get around to writing their dissertation. Deadlines continue to be moved back, year after humiliating, guilt-ridden year. Like my colleagues, like my father, these students outline and make schedules, and you can offer them technologies and helpful suggestions, but something about the project has gone fatally wrong. It is, in fact, ruining their lives.

We all know tenure-track faculty whose jobs depend on completing scholarly articles or books that never get written. They may be researched, even partially drafted, at great personal cost. Over time, while claiming or feigning progress, toxically stalled writers sink deeper into shame and feel increasing loathing for the project, themselves, and the profession. They truly "can't write."

Let go of a toxic writing project before it wastes any more of your valuable time. Yes, this is terrifying, but it is also liberating. It is the best and only way to make room for something more rewarding. That "something" can be a different writing project. But it also can be another academic direction, or a different career that uses the intellectual and organizational skills that academic life requires. We always have other choices, and every one of them will be more rewarding and worthwhile than staying trapped in a toxic writing stall.

A toxic stall drains and debilitates us. Chained to a project we loathe, we can't even imagine alternatives, much less move toward them. We need to clear it away so it won't continue to take us down. If you are in a toxic stall, use your ventilation file to imagine an escape. The least terrifying option is to suspend work on the project and get rolling as quickly as possible on some other quick and fun writing project. Start something simple and rewarding that can get you back into a regular writing rhythm. Get something solid out there for review and revision, and keep choosing truly enjoyable projects. Months or years from now you can decide if you want to reconnect with or reframe your currently loathsome project.

But sometimes this "put in limbo" option won't fully liberate you. You have been chained so long to your albatross that you will still feel the weight of its ghost. If that's the case, you need to symbolically bury your toxic project. I recommend boxing everything up, maybe even including a goodbye note. You may want to throw everything project-related into a dumpster or bonfire, and that's always an option. But if that feels too drastic, just get the project packed up and out of your workspace. Repurpose that space for another project, or for another path or phase of your life.

What keeps us chained to a toxic project? The supposed stakes. They feel so high that we think we absolutely have to do this project or else. We believe we will perish unless we find a way to get it published. We want to avoid the shame and pain of "giving up," even giving up something that is clearly ruining our life. We have spent years learning to navigate the academic system, and we have sacrificed vast swaths of time, energy, and money to it. We don't want to risk "throwing it all away."

This is the same logic that keeps people in toxic relationships. It's much like staying married to an abusive partner because "what would our friends think?" if we got divorced. Our closest associates are people committed to academic success, people who may not respect any other kind of life. This makes it especially hard for us to choose to let go of a toxic writing project, especially if in doing so we might put our academic identity and membership in jeopardy.

I think we need to look twice at what we are telling ourselves. You can't know for sure what will happen if you give up your toxic project in order to move on. Once you free up your mental, emotional, and intellectual energy, you may find options you can't see now, while you are trapped and miserable. If you keep trying to force yourself to do a project you have come to hate, you will end up like the colleagues I've just described—not only unproductive but humiliated.

Question the belief that giving up the project will ruin your life. Also question the assumption that in doing so you will be throwing away years of research and training. Even if it does seem like "career suicide" to relinquish your toxic project, you can challenge the assumption that if you leave academe you will be a failure. Talent, skills, and ability got you this far. Who knows what will happen when you loosen your death grip on what you think you should and must do and instead find out what else is out there waiting? There are many delights outside of the university, delights you may have ignored in your quest to "make it" in academe.

I have freed myself from several toxic stalls by doing two things—boxing up the project (so that it doesn't haunt me) and imagining a happy alternative life for myself. At this very moment I have six boxes stacked outside my home office door, representing six different projects I once started with enthusiasm, even zeal. Somewhere along the way they became uninteresting, even repugnant obligations. I tried the various stall antidotes, including reframing, and sometimes wrote a conference paper or article based on the work I'd done so far. But they were intended as books, and I am so glad that I boxed them up before they took up any more of my time and energy.

What if instead I had chained myself to one or more of them, dutifully following writing productivity steps on a project I did not care about? At best I would have cranked out work that I didn't value. But more likely I would have become unwilling and therefore unable to keep writing, while still being afraid to change course. Eventually I would have been forced to leave (or stay and resent) academic life, feeling shame and guilt because I just "couldn't write." So yes, it takes courage to let go of a project that is turning toxic, but it needs to be done.

In my first job (as a visiting assistant professor at an ivy-aspirational university) I took the risk of abandoning my dissertation to write a new book. At that time I had said all I wanted to say about authenticity and commercialization in country music. The topic now felt stale to me—used up. But I had plenty to say about a more general topic: beliefs about media effects. I was frustrated by popular accounts of media influence and stunned by the combination of ignorance of and snobbery about media (and media studies) that I found at my new university. Freeing myself to write about what engaged me in my current moment led to my first published book on beliefs about the media in modern life.

It was a delight to write—a truly rewarding experience. It helped me get tenure at a different major university with a prestigious graduate program in my field. It remains a book that I am proud to have written. But it exists only because I was able to risk letting go of the "turn your dissertation into your first book" edict. Instead I let myself write about something that truly engaged me at the time, which made it much easier for me to maintain writing momentum.

Years later, a colleague encouraged me to return to my dissertation. By then, fortunately, it felt inviting. After additional thinking and updating, and much-needed revisions, it became my second academic book. Since then I've been able to write and publish books, articles, and essays on topics that really call to me. All because I found ways to let go of projects when they got "in the way."

I have also let myself imagine a contented nonacademic life. This helps me drain some of the drama, allowing writing and publication stakes to feel less high. Especially early in my career, I reduced my anxiety by telling myself that I could and would give it all up. This may have given me the courage to abandon projects that were turning toxic in favor of newer, more engaging writing options.

My advice to let go of a project you've come to loathe may sound cavalier, especially if you are early in your career in these job-scarce times. But sometimes letting go is the only way to make room for something better. It is grueling to be chained to a project that you don't want to complete. If you are truly in a toxic stall, find a way to let the project go. Give yourself the chance to write a different project—or try a different life. Find out what happens when you relinquish your albatross.

W e do our best scholarly work when we can focus on a single project, undistracted by other writing commitments. Few of us have this luxury. Instead many of us have multiple writing projects with overlapping deadlines, forcing us to juggle them (at various stages of completion) in relation to whichever feels most pressing. But for reasons of both productivity and quality, we need to learn how to focus *as if* we had a single project, while still keeping other projects moving forward.

The challenge of multiple writing projects varies across disciplines. The humanities are most likely to offer us single focus; the sciences least likely; and the social sciences fall somewhere in between (more on this below). But we can't just blame our field for our predicament. We often *invite* simultaneous writing into our lives. We say yes to opportunities we don't want to miss, or we agree to write collaboratively with others on different schedules. We miss deadlines so that various projects come due at the same time, or we are unrealistic about how much we can handle all at the same time. We try to get out an extra "quick and easy" something before a professional review, or we get frustrated by our current project and start working on something new without letting go of the old.

Simultaneous writing projects can make us feel productive even if we are stalling and spinning our wheels. They give us lots of ongoing work to describe to colleagues and to list on our annual reviews. But eventually we realize that we are writing-busy but not necessarily writing-productive. The writing projects we actually manage to complete can feel unfinished—rushed out under extreme deadline pressure. Working on lots of projects at the same time is like being a short-order cook, frantically working to keep from sending out half-baked meals without sauce or garnish.

When faced with simultaneous writing projects, you should designate a single primary project—one that gets your A time. This is the project that you have in your project box and keep in daily contact with. Designate all others as secondary projects, ones that you work on (if necessary) in your B and C time. They are on the back burner, waiting for their A chance.

Projects are put on the back burner because they may have later deadlines, or require less effort, or are waiting for additional data, feedback, or a collaborator's contribution. You can turn to them when your front-burner project is in submission or under review. Back-burner projects might also be projects you'd rather be doing or projects that you aren't fully sure that you want to do. Handled skillfully, multiple projects on the back burner can increase your overall productivity. Handled unskillfully, multiple projects keep you overwhelmed and disoriented and may eventually stall you.

Using a front-burner/back-burner system is especially challenging in the sciences. STEM-related fields are collaborative and grant-dependent, so scientists must work in overlapping cycles—developing ideas, applying for grants, creating reports and presentations, writing for conferences and journal submissions, revising and resubmitting until publication. Successful labs do multiple projects with varying elements on different timelines, so productive scientists work on lots of different things seemingly all at once.

But if you look closely, you realize that even the busiest scientist designates front- and back-burner projects—one project is prioritized while the others are kept moving ahead by delegation to collaborators or during B and C time. Efforts to devote A time to multiple projects simultaneously would make things too exhausting, confusing, and slow.

In the humanities, where papers and books are usually single-authored, we have more of an opportunity to focus on a particular research area at our own pace. Humanities types can (but don't always) choose to work on one conference paper or article at a time, and these can then be turned into book chapters or even become the next book. Unlike the overcommitted scientist, the humanities scholar risks becoming bored with this one-project-at-a-time system. When we are immersed in a single topic, it is easy to slow down, stall, or get derailed.

Social scientists are sometimes collaborative and sometimes not. This means that they can become overwhelmed by various projects in various stages of completion *and* they can become bored by a focus on a single topic. But across the academic disciplines, the solution to these productivity drains is the same: designate and focus on a front-burner project while working effectively with back-burner ones.

There are really two kinds of back-burner projects—those that we are forced to put there because we have made far too many commitments, and those that we wish we could be working on instead of what we are writing right now. Both benefit from being kept distinct from a single front-burner project, but each plays a different role in our creative life.

You support a productive scholarly career by identifying research ideas that excite you but that you can't give full attention to right now. Consciously treat these as back-burner projects, and whenever you have insights or find relevant sources for them, put notes and references in a designated file. Back-burner projects can move forward bit by bit, by accumulating material you come across while working on your front-burner project.

Back-burner projects offer fresh options, interesting approaches, and future direction for our scholarly work. They motivate us to finish what we are working on now so that we can start on them next. They energize us, and they reassure us that we will have more to offer once we complete our current project.

I know of colleagues who have nothing at all on their back burner. They may keep publishing, but in an area that no longer excites them. They have chosen to focus on a small corner of the field and write different versions of the same thing. I also know colleagues who have too much on every burner. They always have several possible projects in various stages of development, but surprisingly few of them get completed because they rarely get the full focus they need.

There is an art to the care and feeding of aspirational projects waiting in the wings. You want to stay connected with them, but lightly, just enough to be able to "stir the pot" with additional references, ideas, outlines, or supporting material, but not enough to take you away from your front burner. Zerubavel explains in *The Clockwork Muse* how he sporadically saves ideas and data on a particular subject until, in a few years' time, he has collected enough material to write not just a lecture or article but his next book. By leaving himself notes and methodically organizing and storing them, Zerubavel feeds his back-burner projects so that they are ready for the front burner when their time comes.

If we don't use the front-burner/back-burner system, we can lose months of quality writing time. One of the most common complaints I hear from my colleagues is that they feel too scattered to make progress. My colleagues (especially in the social sciences) often describe feeling frazzled and unfocused in their writing—because they are. They work haphazardly on whichever project is causing them the most anxiety, always aware that they are not really getting anything "out the door." They try to do different projects on different days, or do a little bit of work on several projects during their writing hours, despite sensing that even if they are getting pages written, they are not doing their best work. Their writing demons show up and their writing myths take over. They start to dread and avoid writing time.

By designating a front-burner project while honoring the value of your back-burner options, you engage much more effectively with your scholarly work. It allows you to be proactive, not reactive. You are choosing where you put your time and energy, and you are respecting what good writing requires: regular, relaxed, *focused* attention. This system allows you to give a primary project the undivided attention it deserves.

Designating back-burner projects also allows us to remember, and contribute to, what is waiting for us. In our B and C time we get to check in—are our back-burner projects still bubbling away? Do they need to be reframed, reorganized, or explored for lilt? Stir them briefly, add a spice or two, then let them go back to simmering.

Another way to treat a back-burner project is as the "buddy log" you need to build an effective campfire. Logs burn better side by side, so if you have a big log that you want to burn well, you put a smaller log beside it. When you are discouraged or bored by your single big log project, you can use a back-burner project as a buddy log to get it blazing again. A back-burner project can be used strategically to motivate your front-burner project.

This is what I did with my dissertation on authenticity and commercialization in country music, my first big writing project. Once I figured out how to get myself unstalled, and once I had solved my debilitating structural problem, I found myself working productively for two to four hours each day. My outlines were working, the pages were piling up, and clear and effective progress was being made. Then, out of the blue, I began to wonder about the typewriter I was using.

It was a clunky electric IBM from the 1950s—the model preceding the sleek iconic IBM Selectric. The loud hum, the musty smell, and the feel of the keys were with me every day. This was in the early 1980s, just before the widespread adoption of personal computing. I was handwriting pages, then typing up a first draft, then revising with pen and pencil, then transferring my written-on typewritten pages to a mainframe computer on campus (no desktops yet) for final revisions and formatting. I began to ponder the history of the typewriter just as it was disappearing—what was it like when typewriters were a new technology?

Suddenly all I wanted to do was research the history of typewriters and typewriting. It was an almost untouched scholarly area, one that I had the ideal background for, because my dissertation advisor had done seminal work on the history of new communication technologies. Maybe I could write a quick article, even a book, about it? Obviously that book would be way more interesting and valuable than this boring country music stuff!

I rushed to the library (no Internet then . . .) and was blown away. Deep in the stacks I found an amazing collection of early secretarial training manuals that no one had read in over fifty years. The typewriter had first brought women into the business world! It was the catalyst for a clerical revolution! I found a charming history of the typewriter whose cover showed a toga-clad woman ascending into the clouds, proudly bearing her new typewriter before her as if on a platter. I discovered ads touting the amazing qualities of this new machine that would finally free the world from "pen-slavery." I was hooked. This, not my almost-done dissertation, was definitely the writing project I should be doing!

Fortunately, I remembered that I had felt that very same exhilaration when I began the archival research that led to my dissertation. This helped me understand that if I put "typewriter as new technology" on the front burner, it too could become dull and familiar, and then I might dump it for some other fresh new research interest. So instead of changing projects or trying to do both at the same time, I figured out how to use my new obsession to motivate me to finish my dissertation.

That's when I came up with the concept of the buddy log. In the years since then, I have often been seized by a sudden enthusiasm for a shiny new project. But I have learned to think of such projects as a future reward, waiting for me when I complete my "big log" writing project. A buddy log project helps me keep my intellectual flame alive. It assures me that I have more than one idea in me and that there will be something fun for me to research and write about in the future. So while I was finishing my dissertation, I allowed myself one afternoon (B time) a week to research the history of the typewriter. I skimmed books, created a bibliography, copied pictures, and made a list of questions I wanted to explore. I put everything in an accordion file, separate from my dissertation.

My typewriter project became a B-time reward, a treat, a little vacation for me, when I was in the midst of dutifully writing my dissertation's last chapters. I had been missing the buzz of the new and the thrill of the hunt that I get from archival work. I didn't know then how often this opportunity would come. It was both comforting and energizing to know I had another scholarly project waiting for me once I completed my dissertation.

I didn't ever write a book about the history of the typewriter. But my file on it (which I eventually replaced with a yellow dish pan and then finally a project box) has offered me a trove of material to draw from. I have written several articles about the history of secretarial work, typewriting as a social practice, and the typewriter as a new technology. I still have material ready to turn into a book if I ever feel the urge, but it's not even on the back burner now. Yet it helped me finish my dissertation and led to other rewarding academic experiences.

There are lots of other metaphors we can use to describe how back-burner projects help us stay productive. A back-burner project can be a petri dish—a medium that grows new and different material. My typewriter project helped foster my interest in the history of gendered office work, the unnoticed consequences of the loss of the secretary, and the loss of editing in a world of digital publishing. Back-burner projects are also like sourdough starter—a portion can be applied to help other projects expand and grow. Or like a compost pile, they can fertilize different projects, and like a parts store, they can be shopped for elements to enhance other projects. Much like a buffet, back-burner projects can offer an array of options for lectures, seminars, conference papers, and student projects.

Back-burner projects can serve all these roles only if they are kept contained, simmering, and ready for a stir now and then. Tempting as they can be, you need to stay loyal to continued, regular, relaxed writing on your front-burner project. If I had given in to the siren song of my typewriter obsession, I might never have finished my dissertation or earned a PhD. Or gone on to write more books. I might never have completed any big project, since I am what has been called a "serial enthusiast." To have a productive scholarly career, I've had to find ways to let a back-burner project motivate me to complete what's on my front burner.

Trying to work on lots of different projects at the same time distracts and drains us. Writing about a single topic for years on end bores and discourages us. New projects are the lifeblood of our scholarly careers and the lifeblood of our disciplines. We can honor their importance, and let them motivate us, by learning how to keep them simmering on the back burner until their time comes.

25 } BREAKS, SUMMERS, AND SABBATICALS

W e like to believe that once we are freed from the demands of the semester, we will finally have plenty of time to write, rest, and get lots of other stuff done too. Yet many of us end our breaks, summers, or sabbaticals dismayed by how little we accomplished. We end these much-anticipated periods with regrets, unfinished projects, and unmet goals. Why?

We start our "time off" with vague but sincere plans for lots of writing and relaxing. We want to rest and do nothing, but we also hope to meet tangible professional and personal goals. We want to reach the end of our time off with manuscripts completed, decks cleared, selves improved, and happy memories of relaxation and fun. We also want to experience, if just for a few days, the sense of being off the clock. These goals are all worthy, but they are contradictory. And they don't just happen.

The concept of the Sabbath (the root meaning of the word *sabbatical*) can help us see what we are up against. A true Sabbath is a day when we refrain from all work activities—a day devoted to being, not doing, to resting in gratitude for what is rather than working to create, change, or improve our surroundings. In the Jewish tradition, all such active efforts (including writing) are considered a form of work. Shabbat is to be spent instead in prayer and reflection, as well as in the enjoyment of friends and family.

Shabbat starts at sundown Friday with the lighting of candles and a festive meal. It lasts until sundown Saturday, ending with a ceremony that honors the transition from rest back to regular life. Learning to separate rest from work, and restorative work from dreaded work, changed my life. I was raised without this tradition and believed that I needed to "be productive" seven days a week—how could I possibly afford to take a day off? Choosing to observe Shabbat transformed my understanding of how breaks, summers, and sabbaticals can enhance our scholarly work.

Of course I found it easy to refrain from grading and other dispiriting chores every Saturday—it was a welcome relief. How great to have Jewish tradition ask me to set aside "have-to" work that I didn't really want to do anyway. But what about e-mail and class preparation and the "need-to" work that was piling up? I still found myself fretting and stewing about it every Saturday. Weekends had always been for catching up on what I had been too busy to do during the week. And when writing deadlines loomed, could I really afford to take a day to do "nothing"?

On my designated, sanctioned "day of rest" I still felt like e-mails and classes and scholarship and errands and laundry and cleaning and bills needed my attention, along with family and friends and exercise and hobbies. The thought of losing a full day of productivity was so upsetting that I kept fudging—doing things that weren't really school work but weren't true rest either. By sundown on Saturday I inevitably regretted the ways I'd once again squandered my chance for a full day of rest. I desperately needed respite from "doing" so I could remember how to "just be." In microcosm, my Shabbat struggle mirrors the challenges of academic breaks, summers, and sabbaticals.

I see three basic patterns in how we approach time off in academe. The first is the *workhorse model*: we set up a draconian schedule of writing many hours a day, for weeks on end, in order to meet unrealistic deadlines. The second is a *clear-the-decks model*: we plan to get to our writing once we've dealt with the detritus of our busy semesters. And finally, there's the *vacation model*. We desperately want (and know we deserve) a break from all things academic, and we believe that once we've given ourselves the chance to truly rest, we'll be ready to get some writing done.

Unfortunately, the workhorse model makes us so miserable that we rebel and refuse to keep writing. We rightly know that we need time off, and we resent being forced (by our own plans) to keep our noses to the grindstone. The deck-clearing model is delusional—our decks are never fully cleared. We keep busy doing everything except our writing, as our anxieties mount. The vacation model doesn't work because intrusive thoughts of work cloud whatever fun we are trying to have. We want to forget about play so we can work, and want to forget about work so we can play, and yet we can't fully commit to either.

So what are our options? We don't need to spend our precious breaks forcing ourselves to write, or telling ourselves we will write soon while watching our time leak away, or trying to enjoy time off while still getting stuff done. Instead, during our breaks, summers, and sabbaticals we can and should commit to—and schedule—all three goals. We can give ourselves the chance to write productively, along with the chance to renew our lives, along with the chance to relax into a less pressured rhythm. None of these goals exclude the others. *We can learn to structure our breaks to include all three.*

This is surprisingly challenging. It relies on our ability to treat writing as chosen work, something that can be done frequently, pleasantly, without hostility or force. We can create and protect periods of total rest, and we can incorporate delightful activities, and we can include productive academic writing in our lives. We can do this during breaks, summers, and sabbaticals—and also during the school year.

In other words, we need to recognize that academic breaks are not really "time off." Instead, like the Sabbath, they are "time different." Yes, we are free from teaching and service commitments, but we still have families and friends, homes and hobbies, dreams and desires. We still feel the need to rest and be restored, along with wanting to be productive. But these breaks are also when we lose our writing cover story: that we are too busy with teaching and service to "really write."

So don't re-create the familiar pressures of the semester by planning long writing sessions to meet impossible deadlines or concocting ambitious improvement schemes to change your life. That would keep you too busy to rest. Let go of grand fantasies of what you think you should be doing. Instead, make the time, space, and energy you need for what you actually can accomplish: writing, relaxation, and renewal.

Breaks, summers, and sabbaticals can make it harder, not easier, to apply the craftsman attitude, use the taming techniques, recognize our myths, befriend our demons, and use support systems that work. This is because we think we don't need any special measures because supposedly nothing is now standing in our way. But that is in itself a myth that stands in our way. The reality is that the time, space, and energy we need to meet our legitimate (but contradictory) goals during breaks does not magically appear.

Shabbat teaches me how easily and often my mind fills with work issues—how hard it is for me to truly rest. During my precious Saturdays, I still find myself planning lectures, solving departmental problems, outlining articles, mulling over problem students, and sometimes running errands, cleaning closets, paying bills, or taking care of to-do list items "just this once." Over and over, I have to turn my attention back to appreciating what is going on in the present moment. I am still learning how to put off brooding and planning, errands and to-do lists, for one day a week. I think we all need to learn how to let go of "work-head" and spend time in "Shabbat-head." It is so worth it.

During your academic time off you may be asked to take on minor work-related tasks "just this once." Saying yes will hamper your ability to rest and be restored. So just say no. If you want to make the most of "sabbatical-head" or "summer-head," you can and should step away from department meetings, committee work, manuscript reviews, student advising, and other semester-linked tasks. These seemingly minor teaching and service commitments (made because you think you will have so much free time) become sources of distraction and resentment. As a faculty member you have every right to refrain from doing this kind of work between semesters, during summers, and during sabbaticals. These tasks will wait for you.

I recommend marking the transition between your semester and your break by giving yourself complete rest both at the beginning and at the end of any time off. As with the Sabbath, honor the transition into "time different." You could throw a party, go on retreat, watch movies every day, take a family trip—anything that ritually demarcates the transition.

Take at least a complete day off at the beginning of spring, fall, or winter breaks, a full week off at the start and end of summers, and a few weeks off at the beginning and end of sabbaticals. Make this totally blank time—with no obligations other than to relax and enjoy. Keep it unstructured and unplanned. Just as in a traditional Sabbath, commit yourself to not doing work of any kind. Devote this time to experiencing gratitude and delight for what already is.

These rituals make it much easier to transition into (and later out of) a more relaxed schedule. I have always sacrificed summer teaching money in order to have maximum summer writing time. I used to spend every May and early June in an agitated frenzy, trying to rest and recover but also trying to get nonacademic work accomplished, while feeling like my summer break was "already over." From mid-June through July I was anxious about how much of my writing time was being eaten up by family activities and travel. I might manage to secure a couple of calm, relaxed writing weeks at the end of July, but by early August I was all wound up about how much I had to do before the start of the semester, feeling like I had wasted the summer. I wasn't rested, I wasn't renewed, and I hadn't written enough.

What is the difference between true rest and restorative work? This is a distinction I learned through trying to observe Shabbat. We often confuse the two, but I think we can and should keep them distinct. True rest is unstructured, empty time. It can include sleep, daydreaming, meditation, recreational reading, listening to music, hanging out, or lazing around. It is time without aim or goal or any purpose beyond itself—a time when we are present, content, at peace. It can be spent alone or with others. But it is not about accomplishing anything—academic or otherwise. Time spent like this is increasingly scarce in modern life. It is, I think, what we yearn for when we plan a vacation. But we can enjoy it for only so long.

Restorative work is chosen and purposeful—it involves accomplishing rewarding tasks. It honors our desire to clear out and improve and organize. It is a form of work that feels energizing. Many spiritual traditions teach that such work is to be done with joy, not grim determination. The urge to do restorative work is why many of us use our sabbaticals to clean closets or build decks or enhance our tennis skills. It is an attempt to make things better by making or building or improving or clearing away. It is preparing the garden of self/life/soul. Time for such work is also scarce in contemporary life, but it too is necessary. Academic breaks offer us rare chances to devote time, space, and energy to it.

So what about academic writing? This book is about finding ways to enjoy, rather than dread, writing. The strategies and techniques I recommend are designed to help your writing work be chosen, not imposed, and to feel restorative rather than draining. But that doesn't happen automatically, either during the semester or during your breaks from the semester.

No matter what your circumstances, you still need to secure time, space, and energy for your project. So just as during the semester, identify your A, B, and C energy periods. Plan to write at least fifteen minutes a day, using a project box and a ventilation file. Even though you (supposedly) have so much more time when you are not teaching, stay committed to short daily writing bouts that have a distinct beginning and end. Most of us can't write well for more than a few hours a day, anyway. Remember the importance of knowing where and how you want to start each writing session, and remember to end every writing stint "with juice."

Summers and sabbaticals offer precious opportunities to travel and to take extended rest and renewal time. Should you try to keep a daily writing schedule even when you are on vacation? Is this "working on Shabbat" or not? I have colleagues who enjoy their vacations more if they reserve a little time each day to write, and others who find such a daily commitment ruins their ability to fully enjoy their vacation.

I recommend leaving your options open, depending on how imminent a deadline feels. If "not working" will ruin your trip, devote a defined amount of time each day to writing, then enjoy the rest of each vacation day guilt-free. But if brief daily writing prevents you from being in "vacation-head," then take the whole time off—consciously. I tend to schedule my summers and sabbaticals in weeklong blocks, with weeks of daily writing interspersed with weeks devoted solely to family trips or visits with friends. This works best for me, as long as my writing deadlines can still be met. I stave off guilt by knowing that I have marked off and protected a set number of weeks for writing.

One of the most useful techniques I offer in my workshops on summers and sabbaticals is the monthly calendar day count. I give everyone a calendar and ask them to designate days for total rest, as well as for vacations, travel, or other commitments. Then I ask them to select and count the days when they can schedule two-to-three-hour writing sessions. How many of these writing days will they actually have? The reality is always shocking, because the number of such days is limited. It is immediately clear that writing days need to be honored and protected.

So make and keep a workable, calendared schedule that balances, over the length of your break, all three of your goals. Acknowledge that your energies will fluctuate. Use your most creative hours or weeks—your A time—for writing. Designate your B time for restoring, fun activities and your C time for total rest. You can do this every day, and you can also define different weeks as if they were days—some for work, some for restoration, some for total rest. Mark their beginning and end, and if you are taking a break from your project, follow the advice in chapter 22 ("Working with Stalls") to prepare your writing project for your return.

Honor all three goals by recording your writing time, rest time, and renewal activities. This is a reverse break planner. It is still hard for me to be accurate about how I actually spend my time. Especially during summers and sabbaticals, I find it easy to berate myself for how little I'm getting done. Keeping a detailed record of how I've actually spent my days allows me to see that I really am meeting all three of my goals.

I strongly recommend that you create a summer (or sabbatical) support group, one that is committed to writing but also to rest and renewal. Meet before the semester ends and work together to identify and set realistic goals in all three areas. Commit to helping each other learn how to write, rest, and be restored effectively.

Then set a schedule for checking in, using the guidelines for faculty writing groups outlined in chapter 27. Let your colleagues help you identify what is keeping you from meeting all three of your goals. Listen to their suggestions for how to overcome obstacles not just to writing but also to true relaxation and genuinely renewing activities. Be honest about what happens when your usual excuses (not enough time, too many obligations) are taken away.

When heading into a much-desired break, let go of the delusion that you will have unlimited time. Let go of vague intentions to write lots every day, or once you've cleared the decks, or once you've recovered from the semester. Acknowledge that academic writing is sometimes harder when we expect it to be easier, because we aren't trying to balance it with teaching and service.

Here is a list of ways to make the most of breaks, summers, and sabbaticals:

1. Review and recommit to the taming techniques, including brief daily contact, project box, and ventilation file.
2. Set reasonable goals in three separate areas: writing, resting, rejuvenating
3. Say no to commitments that keep you in "semester head."
4. Devise an energy-sensitive schedule (daily, weekly, monthly) that uses A time for writing, B time for restorative nonacademic work, and C time for rest.
5. Begin and end your break with a defined period of "not working."
6. Devise a calendar that allows you to designate and count days for writing (as well as for rest and rejuvenation).
7. Record your daily progress (time/amount) in all three areas.
8. Share your goals, obstacles, and successes with supportive colleagues, and let them help you figure out what helps you meet your goals—and what stands in your way.

Part Five

··

BUILDING WRITING SUPPORT

Writing can be lonely. The "door that you are willing to shut" on your writing space is also a door that keeps out other people. Even collaborative writing is ultimately up to you. Finding words to say what you want to say, in the ways you want to say them, is a private (and mysterious) process. Generating sentences can be satisfying, but it is still isolating.

Few of us realize that we don't have to do it all alone. Most parts of the academic writing process can be done in the company of colleagues. Research findings, content progress, publication experiences, feelings about your writing—all can be shared. Connecting with other academic writers counteracts the inescapable loneliness of generating sentences. Writing support is tremendously helpful—almost miraculously so.

In this section I offer suggestions for building and using writing support in an academic environment. You can and should overcome the isolation of academic writing by finding ways to connect with kindred spirits. You can form or join a faculty writing group, which is crucially different from a traditional writing group. And you can create writing support at your own university, as I did, using the growing number of academic writing resources available to you.

. . . .

W hen I first went on the job market, one of my professors asked me if I felt ready to "leave the nest." I was speechless—what nest? I had not experienced my PhD program as a safe haven.

But at least in graduate school I was part of an identifiable group—people who, like me, were training to become successful faculty members. So even though my graduate program didn't feel like a cozy nest, it did offer me a readymade cohort group. Some of my fellow graduate students might have become lifelong allies. When we found jobs, we could have supported each other, softening the shocks of being new professors. Over time, we could have helped each other write and publish. In my case, such mutual support didn't materialize—I didn't even realize that it could.

Not everyone goes it alone as much as I did. Some people have PhD programs with friendly peers and available, supportive mentors. Some people form alliances that support their work throughout their academic careers. But that's not true for all of us. Many of us academic types like to spend hours in solitude with our scholarly work. We have found academic success through our own efforts and we expect to "make it" because we know how to work hard all by ourselves.

Traditional academic culture valorizes individual accomplishment, not communal support. Unfortunately, the tight job market means that our peers are also our competition. The process can feel like a zero-sum game, with too many people competing for a limited number of jobs, grants, slots in top journals, invitations to prestigious panels. So for many reasons—experience, temperament, and environment—too many of us stay separate and stoic, maybe seeking advice here and there but rarely committing to consistently giving and receiving support.

Once we are ensconced in academe, asking for advice can feel like an admission of inadequacy. Aren't we supposed to know everything about our profession already? Won't our years of hard work and apprenticeship pay off without help from anyone else, so that we will rise like cream to the top? Isn't academia different from and better than corporate life, where networking and self-branding and strategic alliances are necessary to advance a career?

Yes and no. I'm not advocating taking Dale Carnegie courses on how to win friends and influence people (unless you want to become an administrator), and I'm not saying we all need to join therapeutic support groups (although sometimes I wonder). But we can learn from each other how academic life really works and how to get our scholarly work written, presented, published, and noticed.

Academic alliances help us do better scholarly work because with the help of others we identify interesting areas, research more effectively, write more pleasurably, and find publication more readily. With mutual alliances, we are less likely to get derailed by obstacles to writing. The sense that we are not in this alone, and that our writing trials and tribulations are par for the course, helps us maintain the craftsman attitude we all need to do our best work.

As I detail in the next chapter, on creating faculty writing groups, I'm amazed at what a difference it makes to share the challenges and rewards of academic writing with my colleagues. But overcoming isolation is about more than just joining a writing group. It's also about recognizing the value of giving and receiving academic support all along the way. It's about cultivating mutual connections that help us do our scholarly work.

When I took my first job, as a two-year visitor in a small, conflicted rhetoric department, I was the first woman the department had ever hired, as well as an imposed-by-fiat media studies scholar. I tried to convince my colleagues that I wasn't a threat, while also finishing revisions on my dissertation, teaching new courses, developing a new media studies curriculum, augmenting the library's holdings, and planning a conference, as requested by my chair but resented by the rest of the department. On top of all this, I was starting to write a new book. I found a few friends in other departments and stayed reasonably sane, but I had no true academic allies. I thought figuring out how to be a productive scholar was (and would always be) totally up to me.

My dissertation advisor was influential in the field but, alas, did not feel he needed to actively connect students with opportunities.

He actually told me that academic cream would rise to the top on its own, and he looked down on colleagues who relentlessly promoted their protégées.

I knew a few students from my doctoral program who were junior faculty at other universities, but I didn't know how to establish a connection with them beyond meeting briefly at professional conferences. I didn't want to be a burden, and I wasn't even sure how they might help me. At that time it was all I could do just to stay afloat, much less learn how to collaboratively navigate the new waters of teaching and writing. I didn't realize that all of us deserve to have many forms of support, at all stages of our careers.

Things improved slightly when I took a tenure-track position in an ambitious PhD program at a major research university. But my senior colleagues (all male) were focused on program building and mentoring their graduate students, not on reaching out to a new faculty member trying to look like she already had it all together. My few recent-hire colleagues were, like me, intent on getting tenure—we were cordial to each other and had flashes of commiseration, but we did not become comrades. In retrospect, I think we all believed we needed to maintain a facade of competence for each other as well as for the senior faculty.

Isolation can occur even in disciplines that are explicitly collaborative. In my role as a faculty writing program director, I maintain strictly confidential meetings with junior faculty in the sciences, who are expected to get their research program up and running and funded right away, with almost no guidance on how to do so. They may be the only ones working in their areas, and as freshly minted PhDs they have never set up labs before. They ask me how to find people to work with so that they can apply for grants and generate research to write about. But I don't know their fields, and I myself have never set up a lab.

I also meet with colleagues who come from more teaching-oriented universities or who are returning to academe from other professions. They too need advice on how to write and publish, as well as how to navigate the tenure and promotion process. I can offer general suggestions, but these colleagues need to find successful scholars in their own disciplines to make the necessary connections to grants, conferences, and journals. They need to find effective ways to connect with people in their own fields.

When we "leave the nest" of graduate school we are pretty much out of sight, out of mind to our former professors. They may no longer be available to read and comment on our work, open publishing doors for us, or offer writing insights and wisdom, if indeed they ever were. Our mentors have a new crop of graduate students to attend to, as well as their own research to accomplish. Our graduate school friends who didn't get jobs can't really advise us. Our tenure-track colleagues, in our departments or elsewhere, are pouring energy into their own tenure quests. Who has time to help other people? No wonder so few of us commit to reaching out.

So why do it? Because overcoming isolation—by helping others and letting ourselves be helped—allows us to become happier, healthier, saner, and more productive scholars. Put another way, mutual support makes it less likely that we will become unhappy, stressed, neurotic, and stalled scholars. Creating supportive connections will help you do your research, write productively, publish effectively, and flourish in your scholarly area.

Some fortunate scholars bond strongly with graduate school classmates and use them as sounding boards and advisors throughout their careers. Some also get taken under the wing of a senior colleague who helps them understand the ropes and find the right connections. Such scholars flourish because they have easily available readers for their drafts, advisors for publication options, reviewers to recommend for grants and manuscripts, panel members for conference presentations. The acknowledgment sections of their scholarly books include pages of thanks—a seeming village helps them think, write, and publish.

So how do we do the same, or at least head in that direction? How do we overcome the isolation that we naturally feel—and that can worsen when we change departments or when our department changes, or when we are adjuncts or visitors or independent scholars without people or institutions invested in our success?

The first step is to acknowledge our situation. We are truly on our own when we face the page, the seminar, the lecture hall, or the conference presentation. We are independent contractors building careers in an environment that expects us to already be in the know. But allying with others—helping and being helped—makes the process so much better. Here is what I wish I'd known years ago and what I suggest when I give academic writing advice to colleagues:

1. *Understand the writing and publishing norms for your current and desired position.* Don't stay in the dark or operate by rumor or guesswork. It is totally acceptable to ask departmental colleagues how much you need to publish and where your work should be placed, and whether they can suggest grants to apply for, conferences to go to, journals or editors to contact. And as you advance professionally, remember what you learn and commit to passing it along to others.

2. *Find scholarly allies at your university.* Look for people whose research interests are congruent with yours and who are writing and publishing as you hope to be. Read their work, then take them out for coffee and find out if they are available for informal guidance. Be brief, judicious, and specific in your advice requests, and follow their advice whenever possible. Most faculty members are pleased to have someone on campus who understands and values their work, and many of them are also willing to offer advice when asked.

3. *Contact potential allies in your field.* Whose work do you use and admire? Let them know it: contact them with a brief, specific appreciation of something they've written, and tell them how it connects with your own work. Do this only with colleagues whose work you understand and genuinely value—this is not something you can or should fake. Meet them at conferences, or invite them to serve on panels, or find ways to bring them to your campus. Even the most influential scholars are pleased to have their work lauded, and they are usually gratified by attention from unknown but appreciative scholars at other institutions. It is almost always rewarding to connect with someone who shares your interests and wants to learn from you—just commit to doing the same for them or for others down the line.

4. *When you find allies, ensure benefit.* Find ways to make your relationship intellectually fruitful for them as well as for you.

Be generous in discussing and citing their work; connect them with others you know who might be interested in what they are doing. Whenever possible, send them links to relevant articles and references, and tell them about opportunities you discover along the way that might help them. Academic connections can and should become mutual—make sure you develop from an advisee into a true ally.

5. *Use conferences to deepen scholarly relationships.* Conferences can turn a "scholarly community" into reality—it's your chance for face-to-face contact with people who care about what you know and can appreciate the challenges you are dealing with. Use conferences to make scholarly connections. You will hear stories of colleagues who use conferences mainly to act out in embarrassing ways—don't become one of them. Especially early in your career, it is easy to party, or hide in your room, or hang out only with grad school friends, or spend time only with members of your department. Later in your career it's easy to stop going to conferences altogether. But conferences can be a chance to contribute and connect—and thus stay engaged and productive in your field.

6. Conferences are also a great chance to *talk directly with editors in your discipline.* Academic book and journal editors are resources—smart people who know how to publish effectively in your particular field. Ask them what they are looking for, find out how they make decisions, see whether you can review manuscripts for them—let them help you better understand the process of academic publication. Book and journal editors use conferences to find new ideas, writers, and reviewers, so meet as many of them as you can, and let them tell you how you can work productively with them.

We are in a line of work that perpetually talks about but rarely enacts scholarly community. This can change. To support each other, we don't need to flatter cravenly or network cynically. Instead, we can learn how to make genuinely supportive connections with each other so that all of us can do better scholarly work.

27 } CREATING FACULTY WRITING GROUPS

. . . .

There are basically two kinds of writing groups: those that offer content critique and those that offer support for the writing process. Creative writing programs focus on what is called "workshopping." This is a content-oriented process where participants read portions of their writing to others for comments and suggestions. This kind of writing group is *not* what academic writers need.

We academics have plenty of opportunities to have our content critiqued. When you are a graduate student, your advisor, or another faculty member who publishes where you want to submit, should give you presubmission content feedback. As a faculty member, you can seek out trusted colleagues willing to read and comment on your work and to give you publication guidance. Later the anonymous peer-review process offers specific and detailed suggestions for improved content and style.

What you *don't* need is colleagues unfamiliar with your corner of the field giving you off-the-cuff, contradictory feedback about your emerging content. Do not join a content-critique writing group! You will get much more reliable and focused content evaluation through the traditional peer-review process. What academic writers need (and rarely get) is support for the writing process itself. We need to help each other actually get our writing done. Once it's done, we also need support for getting it revised and into circulation—not just planned, talked about, and agonized over.

As we know, the current academic environment offers us the opposite of what we need to be productive writers. That is why this book focuses on the academic writing *process*—not on advice about style or content. I believe we need to arm ourselves with all the writing productivity advice we can find so that we can succeed in academic life in spite of our writing-hostile environment.

But knowledge does not magically lead to action. Information about which productivity techniques work, and what myths might stand in your way, and how you can approach your demons, won't necessarily keep you writing. Committing to a process-focused writing group—focused on setting regular writing goals and reporting on how and why they were, or were not, met—will help keep you writing.

My own faculty writing group has been meeting weekly for several years. It is one of multiple groups sponsored by TU's Faculty Writing Program. Right now we have a book-writing group (all tenured), a tenure-track group, and two mixed-tenure-level groups that have formed from workshops. We also sponsor temporary groups created for sabbaticals and summers. Each group runs itself, using a version of the following guidelines:

1. *Focus on process, not content.* The group's primary purpose is to help members meet their writing goals for the next meeting.
2. *Stay right-sized and on time.* I think four to six is an ideal number—no more than eight for effective feedback. Meet for no more than an hour at a time, at least once a month. I prefer (and recommend) weekly meetings.
3. *Meet in an academic setting,* not a home or café. Keep the focus on writing, not socializing or venting.
4. *Attend whether or not you've met your writing goals.* If you haven't written, you can use the meeting to figure out what isn't working. If you have written, you can inspire and support others.
5. *Set realistic goals.* Use daily word count, daily pages, times at desk, daily project contact, or specific project benchmarks.
6. *Write goals in a shared notebook.* Each member should leave the meeting committed to a concrete, self-selected writing plan.
7. *Follow a time-for-everyone structure.* Each person has a brief amount of time (5–10 minutes) to share how they did on their writing goals; then group members offer suggestions for what to try next week. No one person should dominate: allow interruptions only to clarify or get back on topic.
8. *Maintain confidentiality.* "What is said in group stays in group," so that every member can be fully honest.

My writing group uses a seminar room in the campus library, and we adjust our meeting time each semester to accommodate changing class schedules. Originally we used a generic writing tablet to keep track of our weekly writing goals; now we use a sparkly lab notebook (stored in the Faculty Writing Program office) to record each person's weekly writing commitment. Each of us ends our "share" by writing down our weekly goals, then sliding the notebook to the next person. This has become our way to invite the next group member to describe how their writing week went.

During our years together, members of my group have weathered numerous challenges—a near-fatal car accident, a child's serious health problems, the death of a department chair, an unwarranted lawsuit, cross-country trips for family emergencies, and other more common but still disruptive crises in work, family, home repair, and health.

Through it all we keep meeting and keep writing. We have supported and celebrated chapters completed, conference papers submitted, articles accepted, columns begun, book contracts awarded, and books published. We have come to know and care about each other, as well as about each other's writing projects. We help each other prioritize and balance our various commitments. We've recognized our patterns of writing avoidance and have seen, over and over, how easily we get deflected and derailed. Basically, we learn from each other what keeps us writing and what keeps us from writing.

We have learned to minimize three tempting distractions during our meetings: content critique, personal therapy, and academic gossip. All groups need to figure out effective ways to stay mostly on topic and mostly on time. If a member needs content feedback, suggest another colleague or offer it yourself, but do this outside of the meeting. If a member needs significant emotional support, offer to meet at another time to talk in depth. If there are juicy academic politics to discuss, feel free to gather later, maybe over food or drink, to dish the details. A successful writing group acknowledges work and life issues but keeps the meeting focused on how to meet writing goals week after week.

My group has members from different but not disparate departments—history, communication, and English. Other groups include members from these disciplines as well as from art history, psychology, anthropology, languages, political science, math, nursing, computer science, and law. While writing requirements vary considerably across these fields, we can still understand and support each other because the writing issues we struggle with are very similar.

I originally believed that writing groups should not mix levels, so that untenured faculty could speak freely without fear of repercussions. But a mix of tenured and untenured members in some of our groups is working out well. I'm glad to know the confidentiality agreement seems to make it possible for a mixed group to work effectively across the tenure line. But I still think it is wise to form academic writing groups with members at similar stages in their career, just to make sure it feels totally safe to share discouragement, frustration, and self-doubt.

If your university does not yet offer writing groups, use these guidelines to form your own. If you join an ongoing group and find out they are doing critique of content, not process, suggest they focus on getting writing done rather than on evaluating what has already been written.

A writing group offers accountability that helps us write no matter what. Group members help us recognize our own patterns, myths, and demons and remind us to use tips and techniques that work. A writing group shows us that we aren't the only ones who get distracted and discouraged, and it offers us the chance to celebrate our successes with people who know firsthand what a struggle it can be to get the words out there.

If you have tried writing groups but have decided that they aren't for you, please try again, applying these guidelines. When I was a stalled and struggling graduate student, I went to an extremely disheartening meeting of a dissertation support group. It was so sad and awful that it motivated me to find my own separate solutions—anything to avoid sharing in their collective amorphous despair.

As an untenured professor I tried another writing group—but its focus on content critique actually hindered my academic work. As a tenured professor I joined a nonfiction writing group, and again, its focus on content critique (the workshopping model) didn't help me do my scholarly work.

Even a well-designed faculty writing group can ebb and flow in effectiveness. One member can dominate and leave others feeling excluded, or people come but don't listen and respond supportively. When people feel stressed and vulnerable (which is how most of us feel about our writing, at least at times), tempers can flare and personalities can clash. If you have joined a group that is not working for you, leave it and form another. If a group stops working for one or more members, a return to the suggested guidelines can help things get back on track.

Please don't let past bad experiences with writing groups keep you from trying again. Membership in a functioning faculty writing group can make all the difference in your scholarly career. I spent most of my writing life going it alone, and even though I still managed to publish articles and books, I now know that my isolation made writing so much more challenging and lonely than it needed to be.

Meeting with my writing group orients, supports, and renews my writing commitments. Getting to know colleagues through their writing process teaches and inspires me, and I no longer feel alone in my writing or in my profession. Adapt the guidelines above to form a supportive academic writing group, and experience for yourself the accountability, inspiration, and encouragement that trusted colleagues can offer.

There are a number of ways you can enhance faculty writing at your university. You can start small by working with a few colleagues to form faculty writing groups within or across disciplines. You can host an informal writing retreat, work to secure a quiet faculty writing space, create a sabbatical accountability process, or develop a writing-supportive book collection in your library.

Establishing a formal writing program at your university is well worth the effort, and because faculty writing programs are both effective and relatively inexpensive, most institutions should support them. A formal faculty writing program involves the elements I suggest above—writing groups, writing retreats, dedicated space, summer and sabbatical planning, a collection of books and articles on writing advice—but in a supported, systematic, visible way. A key resource for designing faculty writing programs is *Working with Faculty Writers*, edited by Anne Ellen Geller and Michele Eodice. This essay collection describes and documents best practices and offers a host of useful ideas from experts in the field, along with evidence-based advice and encouragement. It should help even the most skeptical university administrator see the value of institutionalized faculty writing support.

It has been surprisingly easy and very rewarding for me to develop and direct the faculty writing program at the University of Tulsa. I am a senior faculty member with an endowed chair, so I can volunteer my ideas, time, and energy in exchange for a course reduction. This reduction was not enough release time for the start-up year, but since then it has allowed me to "grow" the program while offering workshops and individual counseling. More extensive or targeted programming, especially at a larger university, would require more course release or a full-time appointment.

I was fortunate to find an ideal home for the program in the University of Tulsa's Henneke Center for Academic Fulfillment. Many universities offer programs or centers designed to enhance faculty teaching, so one obvious option is to create a faculty writing program that is administered through a center for faculty teaching. But writing programs can also be freestanding or, in special cases, added to an established writing center for undergraduate or graduate students.

It may initially seem sensible to combine faculty and student writing support, but I really don't recommend this. Faculty will be unlikely to attend programs designed for (or even connected with) undergraduate or graduate students. There is still so much shame associated with being a struggling faculty writer that it will seem demeaning to participate in a student-oriented program focused on writing remediation. University administrators need to respect the particular challenges of faculty at every stage of their careers and make it possible for them to have the separate resources they need to address their particular writing obstacles.

I developed and proposed the TU Faculty Writing Program as a two-year experiment. I cared deeply about academic writing, but I was not credentialed or expert in it. I had, however, discovered writing techniques that worked for me and that students and colleagues had found helpful over the years. So I read or reread what I thought were the best books in the field and came up with a series of inexpensive program options I hoped might help others.

I met individually with the dean of each college to ensure that the program could be helpful across disciplines. I also met with department chairs to describe my plans and get their advice on what writing support they thought their faculty members most needed. Thanks to the support of central administration, including the wonderful director of the Henneke Center, within a single semester we secured and furnished a space, developed a book collection, and publicized our planned offerings: writing groups, workshops, retreats, and individual consultation.

Colleagues from all four colleges in the university participated from the start. A new College of Health Sciences has been added to our university, and by request I developed programming specific to its particular needs. In general, we continue to build our book collection, offer workshops and retreats, and create and support writing groups that serve both new and established faculty.

The program options that have succeeded for me are working at a growing number of other colleges and universities. Below are brief descriptions of key components of an institutionally supported program at a small university. These can be adapted for larger institutions or be offered more informally at smaller ones. They can be mobilized wherever you are, and the results can be immediately gratifying.

1. Create a *faculty writing resource collection*—books, articles, and websites. The bibliography at the end of this book lists books in our collection, but it is not fully inclusive, and more writing advice books are being published every year. We make our books available for browsing and three-day checkout on shelves in The Garret (see below). We also offer copies of articles and materials from workshops that drop-in visitors can take with them. Not all books that offer writing advice are applicable to academics, so be selective. Make sure to find books that address different disciplines. Suggest helpful resources to specific colleagues, and publicize new additions to your collection to remind people of this ongoing resource.

2. Have a *designated program space* for writing and program-related activities. We were able to convert a small office in our library, just across from the Henneke Center for Academic Fulfillment. The room has sloping ceilings, a single small window, and two walls of shelves. We named it The Garret and furnished it with floor lamps, two small leather couches, a coffee table, and two chairs. It remains unlocked during the day and can be unlocked by a librarian by faculty request at night. An adjacent storage closet was refurbished into a small snack area, with a refrigerator, microwave, and coffee maker. The Garret functions as a specific place to house advice books (checked out through the library system) and other support materials, but it is also a place for individual faculty to drop by, for small writing groups to meet, and for me to offer confidential consultations to colleagues. It is a designated center for all our programming.

3. Offer a *variety of options*. Some faculty might only want to learn a few productivity techniques, others might like to attend

a workshop several times a year. Some want sustained group support for a particular project, while others need individual advice. So offer colleagues various levels of entry, and points of contact, as well as confidentiality. Writing difficulties are not easy to face, and some colleagues will not be willing to attend workshops, join groups, or even seek individual advice. But they will skim books or look at links or read workshop materials that offer productivity techniques, which may help them become willing to try additional options later on.

4. Offer a *series of workshops* each year. I lead four basic workshops, two per semester, that attract repeat attendees as well as newcomers: Securing Time, Space and Energy; Myths We Stall By; Dealing with Stalled Projects; and Becoming a Public Scholar. These work best as small, convivial groups, but they can also be run as larger seminars. Writing programs at other universities offer similar workshops, along with seminars on topics like discipline-specific writing advice, revising and resubmitting journal articles, overcoming procrastination, and working with editors. In the future I hope to offer workshops on digital writing technologies, as well as more targeted options for particular colleges.

5. Many workshops evolve into *temporary writing groups*. Our Time, Space, and Energy participants often decide to meet for a few more weeks to report on how the techniques are working; the Stalled Projects participants keep meeting to help each other revive or relinquish particular projects. Long after the workshops are over, participants let each other know about their successful outcomes. I'm happy to coordinate these temporary groups, but I strongly believe that ongoing writing groups should be autonomous and run by their members.

6. *Ongoing writing groups* are the most consistently beneficial component of our writing program. There is no one-size-fits-all writing group, and groups do not need to last forever. Writing groups can evolve over time to be deeply meaningful to some members, while not enjoyed or needed by others. A faculty writing program director can support ongoing writing groups by coordinating their formation and meeting times,

offering meeting space, advice, and guidelines, and being available to suggest constructive action if there are conflicts. But I think that each group should be allowed to become whatever its current members need and to choose its own members. I encourage colleagues to form or reconfigure groups as needed, so that each of them can create, join, or continue in a group that is right for them.

7. Create a *designated faculty writing space.* Our university library happens to have a lovely, silent, underused faculty reading room that offers an inviting space for faculty to use to write. It has no official relationship to our writing program, but it is nearby and ideal. Designating a quiet place on campus for faculty to come and write for a just a few hours, without interruption, is a simple, visible way to provide institutional support for faculty writing.

8. *Scheduled retreats*, whether for an afternoon or all day, are another popular faculty writing program component. The idea is to combine writing-related information with structured time to accomplish defined writing goals. Our summer planning retreat, held for six hours (9–3 p.m., with lunch provided) right before graduation, has been particularly successful. We offer a review of writing productivity tools and techniques, hand out blank calendars, and then identify, schedule, and commit to writing, rest, and rejuvenation goals for the summer. We include quiet, uninterrupted time to actually start some component of the writing project and arrange for summer accountability options. This means that people leave the workshop with advice, a plan, progress on their project, and support for meeting their summer writing goals.

Writing programs elsewhere offer some or all of these features, as well as all-day lockdowns on Saturdays, overnight stays at an off-campus retreat center, or a monthly all-day writing boot camp. Lockdowns, retreats, and boot camps can offer stalled colleagues a jumpstart, as well as increase a faculty writing program's visibility on campus. They can also offer much-needed escape and camaraderie. But such long, immersive writing "escapes" don't offer ongoing support for what every academic writer really needs: frequent low-stress, high-reward academic writing.

I have tried some things that haven't worked out, at least not so far. In the beginning I scheduled regular drop-in hours, with snacks, at The Garret, but very few people dropped in after the inaugural week. Now I allot several afternoons a week for meetings and appointments and hold them in The Garret as needed. In a larger institution than mine it might be useful to have weekly open-house hours at a program center, with snacks and informal discussions, maybe on a specific topic each week or month.

I had also hoped to identify faculty in each department willing to serve as discipline-specific faculty writing mentors, but few colleagues were willing to sign on to something so amorphous (and uncompensated). Then I realized I needed to keep the process confidential, to protect new, untenured colleagues seeking my help. Now I work with deans to identify actively publishing scholars in a cognate discipline, and I check with them about writing norms, as needed, without violating anyone's confidentiality.

I am still seeking ways to help the most challenging constituency: tenured senior faculty members who will not admit that they are not writing. The current program design seems to work best for new faculty and for temporarily stalled or deflected tenured colleagues in the arts, humanities, and social sciences. I am still looking for better ways to help faculty who haven't published for many years and to assist writing-averse colleagues in the sciences.

One unexpected but successful enterprise has been a collection of academic essays written by TU faculty. This was the idea of a colleague in mechanical engineering who is also a successful science writer. He wanted to create an accessible collection of essays to invite undergraduate students into the scholarly life. Participants in the Becoming a Public Scholar workshop, along with colleagues recruited through word of mouth (including the president and provost), have contributed personal essays to *The Life of Inquiry*, published by our university. It is now offered to prospective students and is being given to all incoming freshmen.

University-wide faculty writing programs can collaborate in other initiatives, including hosting visits by public scholars, offering workshops by experts in academic writing productivity, and sponsoring events to celebrate successful publications year by year. Faculty writing programs can contribute to a more general climate of collegiality, because they offer techniques and support that directly help each of us, in ways that connect us to each other.

I encourage you to develop one or more of these components wherever you are. Obviously it's easiest to create faculty writing support when, like me, you are a passionate senior scholar eager to get things rolling, with administrative support, interested colleagues, and fortuitously available space. But even in—especially in—the most draining and toxic circumstances, it is possible for you to improve the writing climate at your university. Create faculty writing support in any ways you can. The rewards for identifying useful practices and resources, finding on-campus writing spaces, forming writing groups, and offering workshops and retreats are immediate and gratifying. So think small or think big, but get started, and see what happens.

CONCLUSION

....

Universities are finally beginning to recognize the value of offering support for scholarly writing. They are acknowledging that traditional academic culture obstructs rather than promotes scholarly productivity. It is cruel, debilitating, and unnecessary to maintain a mystified writing gauntlet that faculty must navigate all by themselves.

All we are told, basically, is "Write and publish lots, or else." We deal with this unsupportive writing environment as best we can. The stakes are incredibly high; the process remains hidden; there is constant pressure to "crank it out," with shame and humiliation for anyone who stumbles.No wonder so many of us are afraid to ask for help, to admit that we are struggling. We assume that we should somehow already know how to avoid becoming burned out, stalled, or writing-resistant. All this needs to change. And it can.

Productive writing requires frequent, low-stress encounters with an enjoyable project. We can work together to counteract the academic norms that offer infrequent, high-stress encounters with projects that feel like noxious burdens. There are a number of strategies that can help you and your colleagues write more often and more easily, no matter how unsupportive your academic environment is right now.

So use the three taming techniques; secure writing time, space, and energy; and recognize the myths that hold you back. Find ways to maintain your momentum, and seek ways to give and receive writing support. I am constantly inspired by the insights and wisdom that my colleagues offer each other. Our program at the University of Tulsa contributes resources, individual sessions, workshops, and writing groups to their efforts. Real magic happens when colleagues— informally or in structured settings—offer each other their understanding and encouragement.

Everyone benefits when academic writing is demystified. I am glad we are starting to give up the belief that "real" scholars should and must figure it out all on their own. The establishment of a small but growing number of faculty writing programs (along with increasing support for graduate students as well as undergraduates) suggests that we are moving past the damaging practice of letting supposedly "unproductive" colleagues struggle alone in shame and silence.

We may never be able to achieve the idyllic life of the mind we yearned for when we began our journey into academe. But consistent, rewarding scholarly writing is a way to honor and enact the essence of what drew us into our field. Being able to write, often and easily, helps us embody our commitment to scholarship. When we are writing productively, it is easier to teach with energy, contribute to our department, and handle the many challenges of today's often brackish academic environment.

There will always be too many demands, not enough resources, unfair practices, and distressing departmental politics. There will always be reasons to feel that our academic ideals have been betrayed. But whenever we work with each other to recognize writing obstacles and celebrate writing progress, we enact a version of the academic utopia I sought for so long. The suggestions in this book are designed to help you write, but they can also help you embody the most honorable elements of academic life, no matter what.

AFTERWORD } WRITING FOR THE PUBLIC

I include this section because with only a little training and encouragement, many of us can learn how to write about our research for a wider public. This can help us become happier and more productive. It is an option well worth exploring, especially if you are feeling disheartened by the prospect of writing yet another barely read academic article or book.

To outsiders, academics write impenetrable prose about trivial things that they publish in arcane journals to be read by a handful of peers, and so it is all too easy for them to believe that we are overpaid eggheads who contribute nothing of value to the so-called real world. Even people who understand and respect scholarly work criticize traditional academic writing styles as needlessly obscure. Helen Sword in *Stylish Academic Writing* and Steven Pinker in *The Sense of Style* offer much-needed advice on how to make our scholarly writing less clumsy and opaque.

But even the clearest academic writing can exclude the literate general reader. We have been trained to write in ways that keep us from being interesting to outsiders. Eventually this insular, impersonal, and self-referential writing can seem pointless and enervating, even to ourselves. Consciously or unconsciously, we resist devoting our limited time and energy to writing yet another article or book that so few people actually want to read. Why bother?

In contrast, scholarly journalism is writing designed to reach an interested public outside the university. It is writing about research in ways that get our findings and arguments out where they can make a difference. It is science writing, social science writing, and humanities writing that helps the public understand the meaning and value of our scholarly work.

The world really needs scholarly journalism. Especially in an Internet age, the public is being bombarded with persuasive messages written by people who have no accountability to academic values like objectivity, reliability, logic, and validity. As consumers, as citizens, as voters, we are being told self-interested stories and being offered fallacious reasoning and selective evidence, often intentionally designed to prevent understanding. We benefit not only as a society but also as members of the scholarly community when we learn to write in ways that make sense to outsiders.

Scholars are trained to evaluate truth claims and to gather and discover evidence. These academic skills can be used to better examine the world and our roles in it. But for many years, journalists with very little academic understanding have ignored or made sensationalized hash out of our work. Unless we find our own ways to get valid research findings, accurate social science evidence, and thoughtful interpretive analyses out into the world, the public will continue to be misled, while we in the academy remain frustrated by media accounts that distort our work.

Effective scholarly journalism can and should inform public debate. Topics like climate change, immigration, privacy, and technology effects need to be debated with evidence—exactly what we scholars gather and generate. We may have been trained to present our findings to each other in specifically academic ways, but each of us can *also* learn how to offer reasoned arguments and validated evidence to nonacademic readers. In order to do this we need to learn how to write in a different way for a different audience.

After leaving a neuroscience PhD program, I chose to get a master's degree in journalism, thinking that I might become a science writer. At that time journalism training was about learning to write for daily newspapers, which wasn't my goal. I ended up discovering media studies, but I've always maintained a commitment to writing for the general reader. I believe this is a golden moment for many of us to be doing scholarly journalism.

There are narrative strategies that can help even the most specialized scholar communicate to a wider public. But there is also resistance to writing for the public for at least three reasons. First, we don't know how to do it; second, it doesn't count for tenure and promotion; and third, we fear that writing for the public requires us to dumb down or sensationalize our work.

Good scholarly journalism can clarify and refocus our findings, but it should never distort or sensationalize them. Sadly, many journalists and their editors treat academic reports as "news" in ways that misrepresents our evidence and caricatures our work. This rightly angers and embarrasses us and makes us wary of trying to participate in public discourse. So it is very much up to us, as scholars, to find ways to do a better job of reaching the public with what we have to offer. Many of us are already able to explain our work in ways that are accurate but still accessible to a nonspecialist reader. But if we are not, we can find academically trained journalists who know narrative techniques and the ins and outs of nonacademic publishing.

There has never been an easier time to cross over from the ivory tower to the general public. University presses are seeking wider, literate audiences; trade presses are looking for well-written evidence-based writing. While traditional academic publishing is still expected for tenure, some administrators are beginning to recognize the value of public scholarship to their institutions. They are seeing direct benefit to the university when their faculty members write opinion pieces, publish magazine articles or widely read books, or are quoted as experts in their fields. After tenure, there is much to gain and little to lose by becoming a more publicly visible scholar.

Writing for newspapers, magazines, and the book-reading public involves selecting and arranging scholarly evidence to showcase the implications of what we know. When I was in graduate school I wrote a monthly engineering newsletter. I had no training in engineering, but I learned to ask researchers a simple question: "What do you say when someone at a party asks about your research?" From their initial, technical response, I could identify what became the crux of my article. I focused on the implications of their work: What did their findings prove or disprove? What did they make possible? How did these findings change what we know?

Again and again, writing several such stories a month, I helped engineers accurately explain their research so that outsiders like me could appreciate its value. I let them review my pieces before publication, to be sure they were technically correct. My goal was to see that their findings were contextualized in the world, not just in their field, and written in ways that made the implications of their research clear. To my delight, after publication, some of them carried the article with them, so that they could hand it to whoever asked them about their work.

It is possible to describe our scholarship in ways that communicate to a wider public. But we need to set aside the academic writing styles we have been trained to use, and learn instead how to present our evidence and arguments as engaging stories. That is how we tell general readers what we know in ways that make sense to them.

What can you do to become a more public scholar? One option is to make connections to colleagues who are already contributing to public discourse. Are there people in your field who write well for the public? Seek their advice: How did they learn to do it? Is it rewarding? How has it affected their professional reputation? Is it right for you, and if so, how can they help you do the same?

Another option would be to join a group of scholars committed to contributing to public debate. Organizations like the Scholars Strategy Network offer encouragement and training for academics, as well as outlets for essays and interviews. These organizations also keep an updated list of scholars and research areas so that academics can become sources for journalists seeking expert understanding. This is a way to contribute accurate evidence regarding issues of current public interest. Such a network can help you write or place an opinion piece and can connect you with knowledgeable journalists who can describe your work accurately in their stories.

Another option is to work with a nonfiction writer who has appropriate academic training. When you come across an admirable book or article in your field written by a nonacademic, make contact with the author. Freelance writers are constantly looking for story ideas—their livelihood depends on having fresh content to pitch to editors. Especially in today's job market, there are plenty of smart, well-educated writers, often with specialized academic training, who are trying to make a living in a rapidly changing publishing world. These writers know the nonfiction writing techniques that make for effective scholarly journalism. You can partner with them to plan and place magazine articles and books that showcase your expertise.

You can also do it all by yourself. You can write a crossover book for a university press or trade press that is seeking sound scholarship to sell to a wider book-buying public. Talk with university press editors about how your research can be presented in ways that make it interesting to nonspecialists. If you have a book idea but don't know how to develop or place it, there are literary agents who specialize in representing scholarly nonfiction for commercial publication, as well as experienced editors you can pay to help you navigate the rapidly changing commercial publishing marketplace.

There are also online classes and conferences on nonfiction writing that offer techniques, tips, and general orientation. Not all of these are directly useful, since many focus on helping unpublished authors write and place literary nonfiction. Nonetheless, these conferences and courses can offer you narrative techniques and information about commercial publishing practices, even if they are not yet oriented toward helping faculty write about their scholarship for an interested audience.

After all our years of academic writing, we need retraining. Even undergraduates have adopted turgid writing styles that feel safe but work against engagement. When I teach nonfiction writing to undergraduates, I see all too clearly how they have been trained, as we were, to write in the passive voice, in a structured format, without adjectives or descriptions. It takes real effort to let go of the protective shield of distanced analysis and try instead to use an engaging voice to tell accurate and interesting academic stories.

In my workshop Becoming a Public Scholar, we begin by writing opinion pieces for newspapers. We draw on advice from the Op Ed Project,[1] which was originally designed to increase the number of women writing traditional editorials. Their suggestions for writing effective editorials can help faculty recognize and use key elements in any kind of public writing.

Successful opinion essays involve three main elements: anecdote, argument, and evidence. The classic op-ed formula is to open with an anecdote, then make your overall argument, backed by evidence, through several related points. A typical opinion piece also includes

1. www.theopedproject.org.

a "to be sure" paragraph where counterarguments are acknowledged. The conclusion circles back to the original anecdote or central argument.

It's a simple but effective structure. Writing opinion pieces is a great way to break into public scholarship. Area newspaper editors want to make use of local angles and experts, and national opinion editors are looking for credentialed writers who can address controversial arguments with measured opinions and relevant evidence. Unfortunately, academic scholars are trained to write about evidence, but without expressing an opinion and with nary a story or anecdote in sight.

Even the longest nonfiction pieces—magazine articles or books—use the same three basic elements: anecdote, evidence, and argument. Demonstrate this for yourself by analyzing a quality nonfiction article or book chapter for its structure rather than its content. Use three different colors to highlight the illustrative stories, backing evidence, and developed claims. You will quickly see that narrative anecdote (in the service of argument and backed by evidence) is the dominant element in nonfiction work.

All forms of nonfiction writing weave the same three strands together. As scholars, we are always comfortable citing evidence, sometimes hesitant to make explicit arguments, and generally uncomfortable with stories or anecdotes. In contrast, the public is most comfortable with anecdotes and stories, can follow arguments, but is confused by how we, as academics, offer evidence. So our job is to learn how to tell stories in ways that present our evidence effectively, in service to clear arguments.

You can deploy a variety of writing techniques known and used by journalists to tell academic stories. Two helpful books are *Telling True Stories*, edited by Mark Kramer and Wendy Call, which offers advice from professional nonfiction writers about research, organization, and style, and *Writing Tools*, by Roy Peter Clark, which lays out fifty narrative tips and techniques that we almost never use in academic writing but that can help us tell much more engaging stories.

No matter what field you are in, you can't advance public understanding if you write only for academic publication, using a writing style that nonspecialists don't like or can't understand. The world of nonfiction publishing is open to you if you have something smart and interesting to say. If you want to use your expertise, your credentials, and your writing to make a difference in the wider world, I encourage you to explore becoming a public scholar.

BIBLIOGRAPHY

Abbott, Andrew. *Digital Paper: A Manual for Research and Writing with Library and Internet Materials*. Chicago: University of Chicago Press, 2014.

Ballon, Rachel. *The Writer's Portable Therapist: 25 Sessions to a Creativity Cure*. Avon, MA: Adams Media, 2007.

Bane, Roseanne. *Around the Writer's Block: Using Brain Science to Solve Writer's Resistance, including Writer's Block, Procrastination, Paralysis, Perfectionism, Postponing, Distractions, Self-Sabotage, Excessive Criticism, Overscheduling, and Endlessly Delaying Your Writing*. New York: Jeremy P. Tarcher / Penguin, 2012.

Becker, Howard S. *Tricks of the Trade: How to Think about Your Research While You're Doing It*. Chicago: University of Chicago Press, 1998.

———. *Writing for Social Scientists: How to Start and Finish Your Thesis, Book, or Article*. 2nd ed. Chicago: University of Chicago Press, 2007.

Belcher, Wendy Laura. *Writing Your Journal Article in 12 weeks: A Guide to Academic Publishing Success*. Thousand Oaks, CA: SAGE, 2009.

Benson, Philippa J., and Susan C. Silver. *What Editors Want: An Author's Guide to Scientific Journal Publishing*. Chicago: University of Chicago Press, 2013.

Billig, Michael. *Learn to Write Badly: How to Succeed in the Social Sciences*. New York: Cambridge University Press, 2013.

Boice, Robert. *Professors as Writers: A Self-Help Guide to Productive Writing*. Stillwater, OK: New Forums, 1990.

Bolker, Joan. *Writing Your Dissertation in Fifteen Minutes a Day: A Guide to Starting, Revising, and Finishing Your Doctoral Thesis*. New York: Henry Holt, 1998.

Clark, Roy Peter. *Writing Tools: 50 Essential Strategies for Every Writer*. New York: Little, Brown, 2006.

Elbow, Peter. *Writing with Power*. New York: Oxford University Press, 1998.

Elbow, Peter, and Pat Belaroff. *Sharing and Responding*. 3rd ed. New York: Oxford University Press, 2000.

Ellis, Sherry, ed. *Now Write! Nonfiction: Memoir, Journalism, and Creative Nonfiction Exercises from Today's Best Writers and Teachers*. New York: Jeremy P. Tarcher / Penguin, 2009.

Fox, Mary Frank, ed. *Scholarly Writing and Publishing: Issues, Problems and Solutions.* Boulder: Westview, 1985.

Friedman, Bonnie. *Writing Past Dark: Envy, Fear, Distraction, and Other Dilemmas in the Writer's Life.* New York: HarperCollins, 1993.

Geller, Anne Ellen, and Michele Eodice. *Working with Faculty Writers.* Boulder: University Press of Colorado, 2013.

Germano, William. *From Dissertation to Book.* Chicago: University of Chicago Press, 2005.

———. *Getting It Published: A Guide for Scholars and Anyone Else Serious about Serious Books.* 2nd ed. Chicago: University of Chicago Press, 2008.

Gibaldi, J., and D. G. Nicholls. *MLA Handbook for Writers of Research Papers.* New York: Modern Language Association of America, 2011.

Goodson, Patricia. *Becoming an Academic Writer: 50 Exercises for Paced, Productive, and Powerful Writing.* Thousand Oaks, CA: SAGE, 2013.

Graff, Gerald, and Cathy Birkenstein. *They Say / I Say: The Moves That Matter in Academic Writing.* 2nd ed. New York: W. W. Norton, 2010.

Greene, Anne E. *Writing Science in Plain English.* Chicago: University of Chicago Press, 2013.

Hart, Jack. *Storycraft: The Complete Guide to Writing Narrative Nonfiction.* Chicago: University of Chicago Press, 2011.

Hayden, Thomas, and Michelle Nijhuis, eds. *The Science Writers' Handbook: Everything You Need to Know to Pitch, Publish, and Prosper in the Digital Age.* Boston: Da Capo Lifelong Books, 2013.

Johnson, W. Brad, and Carol A. Mullen. *Write to the Top: How to Become a Prolific Academic.* New York: Palgrave Macmillan, 2007.

Kaye, Sanford. *Writing under Pressure: The Quick Writing Process.* New York: Oxford University Press, 1989.

Kendall-Tackett, Kathleen A. *How to Write for a General Audience: A Guide for Academics Who Want to Share Their Knowledge with the World and Have Fun Doing It.* Washington, DC: American Psychological Association, 2007.

Keyes, Ralph. *The Writer's Book of Hope: Getting from Frustration to Publication.* New York: Henry Holt, 2003.

King, Stephen. *On Writing: A Memoir of the Craft.* 10th anniversary ed. New York: Scribner, 2010.

Kramer, Mark, and Wendy Call. *Telling True Stories: A Nonfiction Writers' Guide from the Nieman Foundation at Harvard University.* New York: Plume, 2007.

Larsen, Michael. *How to Write a Book Proposal.* 4th ed. Cincinnati, Ohio: Writer's Digest Books, 2011.

Lerner, Betsy. *The Forest for the Trees: An Editor's Advice to Writers.* New York: Riverhead Books, 2000.

Lindsay, David. *Scientific Writing = Thinking in Words.* Collingwood, Victoria, Canada: CSIRO, 2011.

Lamott, Anne. *Bird by Bird: Advice on Writing and Life.* New York: Random House, 1994.

Luey, Beth. *Handbook for Academic Authors.* 5th ed. New York: Cambridge University Press, 2010.

————, ed. *Revising Your Dissertation: Advice from Leading Editors.* Berkeley: University of California Press, 2008.

Lyon, Elizabeth. *Nonfiction Book Proposals Anybody Can Write: How to Get a Contract and Advance before Writing Your Book.* New York: Perigee, 2002.

Machi, Lawrence A., and Brenda T. McAvoy. *The Literature Review: Six Steps to Success.* 2nd ed. Thousand Oaks, CA: SAGE, 2012.

Moxley, Joseph M., and Todd Taylor, eds. *Writing and Publishing for Academic Authors.* Lanham, MD: Rowman and Littlefield, 1997.

Neal, Ed, ed. *Academic Writing: Individual and Collaborative Strategies for Success.* Stillwater, OK: New Forums, 2013.

Nelson, Victoria. *On Writer's Block: A New Approach to Creativity.* Boston: Houghton Mifflin, 1993.

Ogden, Evelyn Hunt. *Complete Your Dissertation or Thesis in Two Semesters or Less.* Lanham, MD: Rowman and Littlefield, 2007.

Pinker, Steven. *The Sense of Style.* New York: Penguin, 2014.

Rankin, Elizabeth. *The Work of Writing: Insights and Strategies for Academics and Professionals.* San Francisco: Jossey-Bass, 2001.

Richardson, Laurel. *Writing Strategies: Reaching Diverse Audiences*: Newbury Park, CA: SAGE, 1990.

Rocco, Tonette, and Tim Hatcher. *The Handbook of Scholarly Writing and Publishing.* San Francisco: John Wiley and Sons, 2011.

Schimel, Joshua. *Writing Science: How to Write Papers That Get Cited and Proposals That Get Funded.* New York: Oxford University Press, 2012.

Silvia, Paul J. *How to Write a Lot: A Practical Guide to Productive Academic Writing.* 6th ed. Washington, DC: American Psychological Association, 2010.

Staw, Jane Anne. *Unstuck: A Supportive and Practical Guide to Working Through Writer's Block.* New York: St. Martin's Griffin, 2005.

Sternberg, David. *How to Complete and Survive a Doctoral Dissertation*. New York: St. Martin's Griffin, 1981.

Sword, Helen. *Stylish Academic Writing*. Cambridge, MA: Harvard University Press, 2012.

Zerubavel, Eviatar. *The Clockwork Muse: A Practical Guide to Writing Theses, Dissertations, and Books*. Cambridge, MA: Harvard University Press, 1999.

Zinsser, William. *On Writing Well: The Classic Guide to Writing Nonfiction*. New York: HarperCollins, 2008.

INDEX

back-burner projects, 115; buddy log, 117–19; kinds of, 116; metaphors for, 119–20

Becoming a Public Scholar, 145, 147, 155

binge writing, 6, 20, 82

Bird by Bird (Lamott), 69

Bradbury, Ray, 83

Carey, James W., 48, 49

cleared-deck fantasy, 56; and busyness, 58; "free" time, illusion of, 57–59; voluntary commitment, 59

Clockwork Muse, The (Zerubavel), 32, 116

comparison myth, 63, 66; as counterproductive, 64–65; review process, 64

craftsmanship, ethic of, 10–12, 14, 39, 41–42

Crawford, Matthew B., 12

"Dancing with Professors" (Limerick), 11

Elbow, Peter, 68

energy, 15, 39, 41, 75, 149; ABC time, 33–34, 36; A time, 32–37, 85, 114–15; B time, 32–36, 115, 117, 119; C time, 32–36, 115, 117; securing of, 13, 32–37, 44–45, 126, 145

faculty writing programs, 143, 150; all-day lockdowns, 146–47; designated program space, 144; designated writing space, 146; discipline-specific writing mentors, 147; ongoing writing groups, 145–46; options, offering of, 144–45; resource collection, 144; scheduled retreats, 146; temporary writing groups, 145; workshops, offering of, 145, 147–48

feedback: craftsman attitude, 96; as informed, 93, 95; as insightful, 93, 95; as mutual, 93, 95; ventilation file, 94–95

fiction, as art, 10

fifteen minutes a day commitment, 18–21, 24, 39, 57, 85

"Freewriting and the Problem of Wheat and Tares" (Elbow), 68

front-burner projects, 117

graduate students, writing process of, 8

Hemingway, Ernest, 83, 84

Henneke Center for Academic Fulfillment, 142–43

hostile reader fear, 60; depersonalizing, need to, 61; vs. euphoric reader, 61–62; real person, substituting of, 62; support, as form of, 61; ventilation file, as coping strategy, 61–62

How to Complete and Survive a Doctoral Dissertation (Sternberg), 17

How to Write a Lot (Silvia), 9

impostor syndrome: as fraud, 52–54; grandiosity of, 54; inadequacy, feelings of, 53, 55; and self-doubt, 53

isolation, 131–36

King, Stephen, 27

Kingsolver, Barbara, 83

Lamott, Anne, 69

"Learning to Work" (Valian), 20

lilt technique, 78–81, 88
Limerick, Patricia, 11–13
Looser, Devoney, 99
lost trail situation: imaginary conference presentations, 89; lilt, retrieving of, 90; mission statement, 88; old outlines, reviewing of, 88–89; project, reviewing of, 89; reorientation techniques of, 88–92; talking, with others, 89

magnum opus myth, 98; colleague-contempt, 50; craftsman ethic, antidote to, 51; as individualistic, 49; as martial, 49
Mills, C. Wright, 11, 11n1, 12–13
monthly calendar count, 126; as reverse break planner, 127; sabbatical support group, 127
Mumford, Lewis, 30
Murakami, Haruki, 83

Naipaul, V. S., 61
nonfiction, 10
nonfiction writing, 155, 157; elements of, 156

one more source myth, 71–74
"On Intellectual Craftsmanship" (Mills), 11
On Writer's Block (Nelson), 45
On Writing (King), 27
Op Ed Project, 155
opinion essays, 156; elements of, 155

perfect first sentence myth: and editing, 67, 69–70; first drafts, 68–70; and prewriting, 67–68, 70; and revising, 67, 69–70
Pinker, Steven, 151

Power Elite, The (Mills), 11n1
Professors as Writers (Boice), 9, 20
project box, 17–21, 30–31, 42, 119, 126
public scholarship, 151, 156–57

Quynn, Kristina, 17n1

research, 77; draft literature review, 73–74; one more source myth, 71–74; "snare of preparation," 71–72, 74; stalling, as form of, 72
reverse day planner, 23, 25, 34–37, 127; and delusion, 24; self-pity, 24; shame, 24
Rhys, Jean, 61

Sabbath, 121
sabbatical support group, 127
scholarly journalism, 151, 153, 155; public debate, contributing to, 152, 154
Scholars Strategy Network, 154
Sennett, Richard, 12
Sense of Style, The (Pinker), 151
Shabbat, 121–22, 124–26
Sociological Imagination, The (Mills), 11n1
space, 13, 15, 27–31, 39, 41, 44–45, 75, 126, 145, 149
stalling, 8, 145; and loathing, 105, 108–10, 113; psychic resistance, 105–6, 108; structural problems, 105–7; toxic projects, relinquishing of, 109–13; writing lulls, 105, 108
stasis, 105
Sternberg, David, 17–18
Stylish Academic Writing (Sword), 151
Sword, Helen, 151